the Perfect $20 Date

the Perfect $20 Date

DATING SOLUTIONS WITHOUT BREAKING THE BANK

Tomiya Gaines

New York

the Perfect $20 Date
DATING SOLUTIONS WITHOUT BREAKING THE BANK

Published in New York, New York, by Morgan James Publishing. Morgan James and The Entrepreneurial Publisher are trademarks of Morgan James, LLC.
www.MorganJamesPublishing.com

The Morgan James Speakers Group can bring authors to your live event. For more information or to book an event visit The Morgan James Speakers Group at www.TheMorganJamesSpeakersGroup.com.

Shelfie

A **free** eBook edition is available
with the purchase of this print book.

CLEARLY PRINT YOUR NAME ABOVE IN UPPER CASE

Instructions to claim your free eBook edition:
1. Download the Shelfie app for Android or iOS
2. Write your name in **UPPER CASE** above
3. Use the Shelfie app to submit a photo
4. Download your eBook to any device

ISBN 978-1-63047-773-8 paperback
ISBN 978-1-63047-774-5 eBook
ISBN 978-1-63047-775-2 hardcover
Library of Congress Control Number:
2015914401

Cover Design by:
Rachel Lopez
www.r2cdesign.com

Interior Design by:
Bonnie Bushman
The Whole Caboodle Graphic Design

In an effort to support local communities and raise awareness and funds, Morgan James Publishing donates a percentage of all book sales for the life of each book to Habitat for Humanity Peninsula and Greater Williamsburg

Get involved today, visit
www.MorganJamesBuilds.com

Habitat
for Humanity®
Peninsula and
Greater Williamsburg
Building Partner

the Perfect $20 Date

DATING SOLUTIONS WITHOUT BREAKING THE BANK

Tomiya Gaines

New York

the Perfect $20 Date
DATING SOLUTIONS WITHOUT BREAKING THE BANK

Published in New York, New York, by Morgan James Publishing. Morgan James and The Entrepreneurial Publisher are trademarks of Morgan James, LLC.
www.MorganJamesPublishing.com

The Morgan James Speakers Group can bring authors to your live event. For more information or to book an event visit The Morgan James Speakers Group at www.TheMorganJamesSpeakersGroup.com.

Shelfie

A **free** eBook edition is available with the purchase of this print book.

CLEARLY PRINT YOUR NAME ABOVE IN UPPER CASE

Instructions to claim your free eBook edition:
1. Download the Shelfie app for Android or iOS
2. Write your name in **UPPER CASE** above
3. Use the Shelfie app to submit a photo
4. Download your eBook to any device

ISBN 978-1-63047-773-8 paperback
ISBN 978-1-63047-774-5 eBook
ISBN 978-1-63047-775-2 hardcover
Library of Congress Control Number:
2015914401

Cover Design by:
Rachel Lopez
www.r2cdesign.com

Interior Design by:
Bonnie Bushman
The Whole Caboodle Graphic Design

In an effort to support local communities and raise awareness and funds, Morgan James Publishing donates a percentage of all book sales for the life of each book to Habitat for Humanity Peninsula and Greater Williamsburg

Get involved today, visit
www.MorganJamesBuilds.com

Habitat for Humanity®
Peninsula and
Greater Williamsburg
Building Partner

To my beloved late Grandmother,
Charlene Gaines

John 3:16

Table of Contents

Preface   xv

Picture Perfect   1
4th of July Experience   2
Amazing Date   3
Attend an Ice Sculpting Class   4
Attend Church Together   5
Beginners Art Class   6
Botanical/Rose Gardens   7
Bowling   8
Car Show   8
Cartoon Movie Night   9
Casino   10
Chamber of Commerce Events   11
Change a Tire   12
Christmas Lights Excursion   13
Childhood Photo Sharing   14
Collegiate Art Shows & Exhibits   15

Collegiate Concerts/Plays   *16*

Comedy Club   *17*

Crossing Bridges   *18*

Discount Movie Tickets   *18*

Dog Park   *19*

Duck Feeding   *20*

Easter Egg Hunt w/Lover's Coupons   *21*

Fast & Fabulous   *22*

Favorite Movie Night   *23*

Game Show Taping   *24*

Happy Hour with Appetizers   *25*

High School Sporting Event   *26*

Hiking Excursion   *27*

Horseback Ride   *27*

Horticulture Class   *28*

Kayaking   *29*

Living Escape   *30*

Living Night Club   *31*

Local Arcade   *32*

Local Fitness Center (Gymnasium)   *33*

Local Theatre Plays/ Musicals   *35*

Lover's Scavenger Hunt   *35*

Martial Arts Movie Night   *36*

Neighborhood Zoo   *37*

Paddle Boats   *38*

Photo with Easter Bunny   *39*

Photo with Santa   *40*

Pizza n' $2 Buck Chuck   *41*

Pottery Class   *42*

Rock Climbing   *42*

Rock Exploration   *43*

Salsa Dancing   *44*

Scenic Walking Tour (San Francisco)   *45*

Sewing Class   *46*

Snow Play Date   *47*

Summer Concert Series (FREE)   *48*

Sunset at the Marina   *49*

Swimming Class   *50*

Teach Him How to Bake a Cake   *51*

Volunteer at Neighborhood Shelter/Non-Profit Facility   *52*

Wine Tasting   *53*

Yacht Dinner Cruise   *54*

Zumba   *55*

Attractions   **57**

Adventure Landing   *58*

Adventure Park   *58*

African Wildlife and Safari   *58*

America's Stonehenge   *58*

Balboa Segway Tour   *59*

Boardwalk Amusement Park   *59*

Buccaneer Bay Waterpark   *59*

Cemetery After Hours   *60*

Conservation Center   *60*

Comedy Pet Theatres   *60*

Dinosaur Ridge   *60*

Empty Grave Haunted House Experience   *61*

French Quarter Phantoms   *61*

Ghost Tour   *61*

Harper Fowlkes House   *62*

Holocaust Memorial   *62*

Illusions 308   *62*

Joe Dumar's Fieldhouse   *63*

Kennedy Tour   *63*

Lake Arrowhead Resort   63
Living Coast Discovery Center   63
Mission Beach Attractions   64
National D-Day Memorial   64
Nottoway Plantation and Resort   64
Pirate Ship Adventure   65
Planetarium   65
Polynesian Adventure Tour   65
Popcorn Palace   66
Railroad Tunnel   66
St. Joseph's Plantation   66
Wilderness Adventure   67

Indoors   **69**
Air Museum   70
Art Museum   70
Atomic Testing Museum   70
Ballet/Musicals   71
Car Museum   71
Corvette Museum   71
Cotton Museum   71
CSI (Crime Scene Investigation) Museum   72
Earth Science Museum   72
Go Kart Racing   72
Ice Skating   73
Indoor Surfing   73
Laser Tag   73
Lightner Museum   74
Mechanical Museum   74
Museum of Sex   74
Osteology Museum   75
Plant Museum   75

MLB Stadium Seats   *98*

Minor League Sporting Event   *99*

NBA Stadium Seats Game Day   *99*

By the Bay   **101**

Adventure Diving   *102*

Aquarena Center   *102*

Casino Cruise   *102*

Catamaran Cruise   *103*

Deep Sea Fishing   *103*

Dining Cruise   *103*

Hornblower Cruise   *104*

Hydro Biking   *104*

Manatee Tour and Diving   *104*

Ocean Explorer Cruise   *105*

Riverboat Cruise   *105*

Scuba Diving   *105*

Sportfishing   *106*

Whale Watching Cruise   *106*

Preface

Contrary to popular belief, women are the simplest creatures on earth. Most often it's not how much you spend, it's the amount of thought and attention that goes into what it is that you do that makes each moment special. It's the attention to detail.

It was late Summer, early Fall 2008, and I was dating this guy. Everything we did as a couple involved spending money (well, almost everything).

I remember this one particular sunny summer afternoon as if it were yesterday. We travelled along a stretch of California's Highway 41 for several minutes deciding what to do. Everything we could possibly think of involved spending lots of money. That's when the thought occurred to me—

What if we weren't a fortunate couple? What would life look like if we weren't blessed to do what we wanted, when we wanted? Regardless of price. What if either of us were on a fixed income? Would that mean we couldn't live life to its fullest potential?

So then I'd asked him, "What would you do if you only had $20 to spend on a date with me? What would we do?"

He paused, obviously quite puzzled. He replied, "I don't know!"

Twenty dollars seemed like such a miniscule amount of money, he couldn't fathom it.

Unfortunately, for many financially challenged Americans it's a harsh reality. Unless your employment is recession proof, you're probably one of the millions of Americans who's been impacted by this recession. For many of you, your romantic life has probably suffered too.

In that moment it became my mission to find the **Perfect $20 Date** (dating scenario).

(Disclaimer—The premise of this book is to inspire the reader to use his/her imagining faculty to create the perfect dating scenario. Some of the dating scenarios described in this book are region specific and may not be available in your area. A price point for dating scenarios described herein does not exceed $20 per person. However, prices are subject to change without notice. For a list of scenarios in your region you may visit our website. You may also visit our Facebook/Twitter page.)

Picture Perfect

❈ 4th of July Experience ❈

It's Independence Day and everyone is filled up on hot dogs, beer, and burgers. The day is winding down but there is one more tradition to experience: fireworks! Grab your date by the hand and lead them to a quiet spot where you can enjoy the show together.

Sneaking away from the group of family and friends to watch the display together can turn a routine tradition into a romantic night for both of you. Find a vantage point that is secluded but gives you a clear view of the sky. This will be you and your date's special place where you can return to in future years.

Bring a blanket to spread out on the ground and stretch out together, looking up into the night sky as it's set on fire in colors of gold, red, green, and blue. Don't try to talk over the noise of the explosions, just lie together holding hands and experiencing the beauty of the show. Share a drink together as you watch.

Point out which types of fireworks you like the best, the large bursts that radiate outwards like a miniature sun, or the cascading drizzle of color as a rocket detonates then drapes elegantly back towards the earth. After the grand finale you can continue lying quietly together looking at the stars and talking about your favorite 4th of July's as children. Take the time to build a memory of this 4th that will be just as special to each of you as your childhood reminisces are to you.

❋ Amazing Date ❋

Does the usual date, such as an elegant dinner or quiet movie, not interest you? Would you and your date prefer to be outside, enjoying nature, biking or hiking, or doing other outdoor activities rather than staying inside? Captivated by the hit TV show, "The Amazing Race"? Then how about creating your own race!

Start out by having each of you write down several places you'd like to visit and explore, as well as the routes that you will take to get there. Alternatively, one of you could figure out the attractions to visit, and the other would take care of the logistics and transportation. To make it even more exciting, keep your destinations a secret and surprise your date!

Then, it's off to your adventure! Use your guidebooks and only the items, clothing and currency that you have brought with you. Try to complete each challenge within the time limits you have set for each other. Follow the markers that have been placed along the way. Create an adventure within an adventure while hiking along a mountain trail, climbing that rugged terrain or crossing still waters (or whitewater rapids!).

Solve the puzzles that you have created for each other, including roadblocks, hazards, and obstacles. Add a little spice to the clues and riddles you've left behind. The best part is once you've completed assigned tasks, you can give each other a prize at the end for a race (and romantic adventure!) well run.

❄ Attend an Ice Sculpting Class ❄

You don't need a chainsaw or an ice pick for your next date, but you do need a sense of adventure and a sturdy pair of gloves.

Don't worry, we're not suggesting you reenact a scene from your favorite horror film. I'm suggesting an ice sculpting class!

Ice sculpting may seem daunting at first, but a good class will leave you both marveled and inspire you towards creating your own frozen piece of art. Emphasizing safety is always first. Chipping into that first small block of ice may appear challenging but keep a good sense of fun and before you know it you'll start seeing something materialize before your eyes.

The first step isn't sculpting at all but rather drawing. 3D visualization is the foundation of the instructor's masterpiece. Carving with a plan! As a way to interact with your date during the class ask them what they would like you to carve for them. Put your effort into a design knowing you've got to impress your date!

Who knows—you may have the opportunity to present your date with an actual ice sculpture for Valentine's Day, Birthday, Anniversary, or another special occasion. You may get the chance to carve it yourself. Your first attempt or two won't look much like what you envisioned but keep at it and you might surprise yourself. Even if you just start with a cube or a pyramid it is a challenging skill that will definitely fill you with a sense of accomplishment to learn. And tackling challenges together and overcoming them is one of the best ways to grow together as a couple.

❁ Attend Church Together ❁

One of the most important parts of our everyday lives is what we believe and put our faith in. Our worldviews and what we believe in shape everything from what we do to who we spend our time with. More than likely if you are in a committed relationship your partner shares the same faith and values as you do, and if you are just starting out in a relationship finding out your significant other's views on these matters should be a priority. Attending church together can be a deeply bonding spiritual experience and a great way to learn more about each other as you learn more about life.

Christian, Protestant, Jehovah's Witness, or Muslim, each religion is unique and very different. But across the board the opportunities to get involved in community service and volunteer work together through your church are plenty. From youth programs to homeless outreaches the experience of volunteering to help others in need takes on value far beyond just being a date.

Churches also often have young couples' nights which are a great way to spend an evening enjoying food, fun and fellowship with other couples of similar age and faith. These social events are low stress, high energy, and perfect for cultivating a spiritual bond without the structure and rigidity of a traditional church service setting.

If your date is of another faith or denomination, make the effort to visit their place of worship and learn more about what they believe. We often form biases in our own mind well before actually experiencing a new belief system for ourselves. So keep an open mind and understand why the values and beliefs that might be different than yours are important to your date. Above all remember there is a reason you are in love or falling in love with this person, and their faith plays a key role in who they are just as it does in who you are.

❈ Beginners Art Class ❈

For your next date take an art or painting class together. Whether it's an intro to drawing class or painting 101 finding your unique artistic voice and watching your date find theirs is a rewarding experience. Expressing yourselves through a creative outlet can work to bring you closer together and help you learn more about each other in a fun and laid back environment.

One of the best ways to make your art class experience more romantic is to create something for your date. Whether your portrait drawing is of her or your painting is of his favorite vacation spot, having them in mind while you create your piece imbues each stroke of the pencil or paintbrush with thoughtful care.

Decide on a subject you both love, and then work as a team to create the backdrop, the colors, and the texture. Mixed media art, Photoshop, or your local art store is a great place to get started. For example, if you are creating a seascape, one of you can paint the sky and the waves while the other creates the boat or aquatic life out of found materials. Your unique skill sets coming together to make something greater is the perfect analogy for a healthy relationship. Learn what your partner's strengths and weaknesses are during the class and look for ways to complement them. Coming alongside to help them with a watercolor technique you mastered quickly while also asking for advice on pen and ink drawings they are good at is a great way to establish a give and take in the class between the two of you. Accentuate this experience with a personalized keepsake that you've created together. In the end, it's just as much about creating a beautiful relationship as it is creating beautiful art.

❀ Botanical/Rose Gardens ❀

Take in the smell of sweet exotic flowers at the botanical gardens. Stop to admire koi ponds and bamboo sprouts, taking in all the wonderful splendor of your local botanical garden. From local endangered flowers, grasses and shrubs to imported exotic collections you can sample a bit of everything wild and beautiful nature has to offer with your lover on your next date.

Pick a time to visit early in the morning before the foot traffic has picked up. Stroll leisurely through the paths and across brooks as you listen to the birds chirping merrily in the trees. Stop off at a bench for a few moments to sit quietly, holding hands and breathing the fragrant air. Make sure to visit the sections of the garden that include non-native plants and learn a bit about the fascinating flora found in other corners of the country and world.

A counterpart to botanical gardens is the aromatic rose gardens. Here you will find roses a surprising variety of shapes and colors. Read about the origins of their breeding together and view some of the greatest creations ever crafted by horticulturists. After you leave make sure to stop and pick up a few roses to bring home as well. Setting them on the windowsill and smelling them every morning when you wake up will remind you of the beauty of the gardens, and of the quiet and tender times you've spent there with your lover.

❈ Bowling ❈

Find your ugliest pair of shoes and grab a wrist brace. It's not revenge of the nerds, it's bowling night! Taking your date bowling is an American tradition and 10 pins worth of fun.

2 for 1 coupons for shoes and lanes are often available. Check your local alleys for specials, whether it's shoes free on Wednesdays or Thursday night half off specials.

Check with your local alleys not just for savings, but for theme nights. Disco bowling or glow in the dark bowling is still alive and kicking, and a great way to spice up your night out. Inquire about duckpin or candlepin bowling as well. These are variations where the pins are a different shape, the bowling balls are smaller, and you get three rolls a turn. This can be a great challenge from regular bowling and perhaps start a new tradition with you and your date.

If neither of you is particularly adept at bowling, ask about getting a lane with bumpers. A lot of alleys will only give these out to children but if it's a slow night you might get lucky. Putting up the bumpers can take a lot of the frustration out of the game and help you both focus more on having a good time together rather than improving your score. Making this the perfect All-American date night.

❈ Car Show ❈

Visit a local car show on your next date to see some classic automobiles, learn some history of different car manufacturers, and talk with industry leaders about the newest advances in technology. Car shows are a fun and friendly environment for you to spend the day lazily walking together and spending time in each other's company.

A good car show will have several components. Classic cars, modern cars, games for the kids, and a grill all make for a busy but laid back atmosphere. Grab a burger and a beer and munch away happily, listening to the sounds of owners firing up their engines for a test ignition. Get a photo with your date next to a classic 1960s Jaguar or a Lamborghini. Visit local vendor booths where you can sample some of the local crafts and cuisine.

A modern car show is a fun place to see what's coming next to a freeway near you. From concept cars to new production models you can get a look at sleek leather interiors and cutting edge design. Check with the event program to see what sorts of entertainment options are offered as well. Whether it's a live band or a racetrack demonstration of a new model, there is always something new and interesting to see. It's a great way to get out and try something new with your date!

❄ Cartoon Movie Night ❄

Wish you were a kid again? Do you wish you could partake in the classic Saturday morning ritual of watching cartoons? Or the excitement of going to see the newest Disney or Pixar animated film in theaters? Chances are so does your date, and a cartoon movie night is a fun throwback to your childhood that makes for a great evening.

Back when movies were first being shown in theaters it was common for a cartoon or two to run before the featured presentation. Pixar has continued this tradition with its short animated films before the feature length movie starts, and you can too! Pick a few of your favorite cartoons, from Looney Tunes to Mickey Mouse, to watch before the movie plays. This gets you laughing early and in the mood for a night of old-fashioned fun.

Modern cartoons come in all shapes and sizes for anyone's taste. From the innocent adventure of The Incredibles to the pop culture heavy Shrek to the off color humor of a Family Guy film you might be surprised just how relevant cartoons are in modern comedy. If you have a service like Netflix, iTunes, or Amazon Prime handy, ask your date what their favorite cartoon was growing up, and then try and surprise them by pulling it up to watch at a moment's notice.

Complete the theme of the evening with snacks from your childhood Saturday mornings. Have a bowl of cereal for dinner along with chocolate chip cookies and a glass of milk. We all wish we could be a kid again, use cartoon movie night to give that experience to your date.

❋ Casino ❋

Winner winner, chicken dinner! Whether your game is blackjack, the slots, poker, or craps you and your partner can have a high energy and thrilling night out for your next date at the casino. Heading to the casino for an evening is a great way to live out some of your high roller fantasies, and enjoy the other amenities and attractions offered as well!

Many casinos don't have a dress code, but this is a special night so grab your tux or cocktail dress and make a grand entrance together. Set a limit for what you will gamble, the focus should be on having a great time together and not worrying about your chip stack! No matter your budget though, playing the part of the high roller with swagger and confidence is a fun experience and a great inside joke for you and your date.

One of the best tricks for having a great time at the casino without blowing your budget is to take advantage of the amenities but limit your gambling money. Casinos count on you spending some extra change at the tables so they drop the prices of their rooms, restaurants, and amenities. If you and your date can exercise self-control and not overspend at the poker tables you can take full advantage of all the fun and entertainment without going home with empty pockets!

When you've tired of the games (though hopefully not because of losing!) check what other amenities the casino has to offer. Catch a live show or comedy act, or take a dip in the pool to cool off from the excitement of the casino floor. The casino really is a one-stop mini-vacation experience.

*(Tip: 1st time visitors at most casinos who apply for casino players card will receive **FREE** cash—Cost of this date **FREE*****)*

❀ Chamber of Commerce Events ❀

One source of great events for dates you may not readily think of is your local Chamber of Commerce. As part of giving back to the community, chambers everywhere put on events that promote local businesses and offer wonderful community outings with food, music, and culture. Take your date to your next chamber sponsored festival for an awesome way to get to know each other.

A festival is the perfect venue to become more acquainted with someone in a relaxed and fun setting. Whether it's bar hopping on a pub crawl or sampling downtown's finest restaurants at a tasting event you can get to know a lot about your date's favorite tastes and personality while learning a bit about culinary tastes too! Live music often accompanies these events, so stop and find out what type of bands they prefer and stick around for a few numbers, taking your time to soak in the local culture.

The relaxed nature of an open community festival creates the perfect environment to talk and laugh with your date. Grab some cotton candy and soda from a vendor and satisfy your sweet tooth together, while chatting about your favorite summertime haunts as children where you would sneak off for ice cream and sweets. Participate in carnival style games together, pause to watch the street performers on display during this high traffic time, and settle in for a few hours of nighttime conversation at your favorite downtown wine bar. There are limitless things to do and experience, and seeing them all with that special someone makes the day all the more magical.

❄ Change a Tire ❄

Changing a flat is a vital skill to have if you do much driving. Being stranded on the side of the road without being able to get yourself to the next auto shop can be a frightening ordeal. If your partner isn't the handy type and needs to learn how to change a flat, take the opportunity to teach her and turn the experience into a fun afternoon together.

Safety is always the first step. While this should be a fun and enjoyable time together learning something new, that can quickly be ruined by a carjack that wasn't placed properly and failed. Make sure she knows that now, and in the future, the first and most important step to any auto work is being safe.

Once you have all the tools together for the tire change, demonstrate to her how to place the jack, raise the car, and start the tire change. Depending on her strength, teach her a couple of tricks for applying more torque to the lug nuts so she can get the tire off when needed. Make sure to take your time with each step and listen to her questions or comments.

Once you've demonstrated all the proper steps, have her repeat them with supervision. Make sure to compliment her when she's done and let her know you hope she's there for you when you get in a jam! Take the newly fixed tires out for a spin and grab dinner, or dessert...hopefully her newfound skills won't come in handy just yet!

❄ Christmas Lights Excursion ❄

Seeing the Christmas lights and decorations every year is a time honored tradition in many families. Husbands and wives, boys and girls all pack into the family car and head down the street to see what their neighbors have put together for the season's electric light spectacle. This is also a great activity for dating couples, whether you've been together for many Christmases or this is your first.

Driving from street to street is a great way to catch as many lights as possible, but if the weather permits, consider taking the trip on foot. Bring along a thermos of hot chocolate and some Christmas cookies or fudge to snack on. Hold hands as you stop and take in each Santa display or nativity scene.

Venture outside your neighborhood for a beautiful Christmas lights display. Take a trip downtown to see what local businesses have put together in their storefronts. Stop and build a snowman together (make sure to bring the carrot and coal for his nose and eyes!) or make snow angels and lie for a moment together looking up at the winter sky.

If you and your partner have been together for multiple Christmases talk about your favorite moments from years past that you've had together. Reminisce about something funny?

Or the time the car got stuck in the snow? If this is your first Christmas together get to know how your date's family used to decorate their house and if annual sightseeing of the lights in town was a tradition for them. Christmas is a time for lovers, and the magical display of lights is a beautiful backdrop to your romance.

❋ Childhood Photo Sharing ❋

One of the best parts of getting to know someone in a relatioship is finding out about their childhood. Everyone's is unique, but finding the common ground in your childhood backgrounds can really create a strong bond between you and your partner. One great way to facilitate this is to take an evening and share photos from your childhood photo albums.

Let's face it, eventually your mothers will try and embarrass you in front of your date by pulling out the photos of you in the tub, wearing that horrible tutu, or sporting the bowl cut you begged her to let you get when you were 12. Head her off on your own terms and take ownership of your cute or humiliating childhood photos. Start with the baby pictures which are sure to get a reaction from your date, and work your way through to your teenage years. Take time to elaborate on different places you went, or things you experienced that show up in the photos. This time is about more than just flipping through some snapshots, it's a chance for you to tell the story of your life and to hear your lover's as well.

If your photos are just in a binder and not presented in any special way, suggest that you and your partner spend an evening being crafty and creating a scrapbook from your childhood pictures. Incorporate the stories from each photo on the page and compare books when you're done. The similarities of your childhood may surprise you.

Whether you were sporting bellbottoms, fanny packs, perms, or dorky glasses your childhood is something your partner wants to learn about in order to better understand who you are. Enjoy the fact that they accept you for you, whether that's embarrassing or adorable.

❊ Collegiate Art Shows & Exhibits ❊

If you and your date appreciate modern art and want a chance to view some up and coming artists for free, check out your local collegiate art shows and exhibits. At least once every semester the students will take the compilation of their classwork and put it on display for the general public to view and appreciate. This is a perfect budget conscious date that will expose you to some of the finest talent in the young art scene.

One of the best aspects of a collegiate art show is the variety. Students will simultaneously display art differently, unique to their individual personality. From photography to graphic design to painting and mixed media you can see snapshots of almost every medium and genre at a college show.

Keep an eye out for graduate student exhibitions as well. These often showcase a larger body of work per student and have a more unified theme that can tie together multiple mediums and messages. Seeing a graduate student's thesis work can be a real treat as they have had the time and experience to hone their craft and really devote their creative energy to exploring new and experimental ideas.

Supporting your local college by attending shows is another great reason to visit with your date. Students want and need to get as many fresh eyes and opinions on their work as possible so they can grow and improve. Look for a comments box at the beginning or end of the exhibit. Let a young artist know what you appreciated about their work and how it impacted you. Who knows, you and your date could have the privilege of spurring on the next great young artist.

✹ Collegiate Concerts/Plays ✹

If you are looking for an alternative to your classic theater or concert experience, check out the showings at your local college. College Theater and concerts are a great way to support up and coming artists and have a wonderful time at a show as well. Tickets are usually a bit cheaper than your standard theater and it's always worth your money when you can take in a bit of culture with your date.

College Theater ranges from modern plays, to originally written productions, to classic and adapted Shakespeare. No matter what your taste you are sure to find something to fit it. And though these thespians may not be on Broadway yet you might be surprised at how good they are! They put the time and effort in like any performers and with the guidance of their professors a well-produced collegiate play can be a real treat.

College orchestras also put on concerts several times a year and this is a perfect gateway for you and your date to step into the formal scene of orchestra. Iron your best black suit, and crease your socks. Ladies, wear that formal gown you never thought you'd have occasion to use and enjoy being treated like a queen for the evening. Formal occasions can be just as fun as kicking it on the beach barefoot, you just need to be in the right mood!

Regardless of your taste, being able to appreciate the arts together is something that will be valuable to your relationship for years to come. And getting a sneak peek at the Broadway and Philharmonic stars of tomorrow is an enriching and exciting experience!

✿ Comedy Club ✿

A great way to spend a night on the town is to visit an open mic night, amateur comedy night, or talent show at your favorite bar or restaurant. Some bars have these quite regularly so you should easily be able to find an event going on near you. Do a little research on your date's favorite type of show, whether it's music, comedy or variety and plan a night for that.

Open mic nights are a great way to hear some new and exciting talent without the expectations of undivided attention a traditional concert brings. Enjoy conversation with your date over drinks as various singers and bands showcase in the background. If there is dancing, invite your date onto the floor for one of the more upbeat numbers, and stay on the floor for a more intimate slow dance.

An amateur comedy night can be a great way to unwind with your date and just have a genuinely good time. Many of the comedians might be new and their material unpolished, but usually there are a few headliners at these events who are very good and are sure to get you both laughing. A comedy night can be one of the best and easiest ways to show him or her a good time.

Talent shows may not be as common but they can be just as much fun. From singers, to jugglers, to magicians a good talent show has something for everyone and is sure to please no matter what your date's interests. Seek out a talent show that is advertising a wide range of acts to help spice up any mundane dinner date into a night of extravagant showmanship.

Of course if you are the talented type the ultimate move is to secretly enter the open mic night or talent show yourself without telling your date. Then when your name is called make sure to dedicate your act or performance to your date and let them know you are thinking of them. No matter how you perform this brave gesture is sure to cap off a fun and special night with a personal touch of romance.

✻ Crossing Bridges ✻

Set aside your next date for a quiet and intimate evening spent together outside. Forget about what movie to see, what restaurant to visit, or what show to go to and enjoy the sunset and the peaceful evening air strolling down the sidewalk and over a bridge.

Pause to take in the water and the orange and purple evening rays playing across its surface. Spend time just holding hands and talking, bonding and deepening your relationship. Not every date needs to have excitement and thrills; sometimes just the simple act of being together can be all you need.

Open up and talk about your dreams and aspirations. Make plans together for the coming year and set goals for the two of you to accomplish. As the light dims and the night sets in, make your way back home under the streetlights and appreciate the quiet times you can spend with your partner. Enjoy peace and tranquility with your potential soul mate.

✻ Discount Movie Tickets ✻

If you're looking to go to the movies on your next date but don't want to shell out the cash for the ever rising cost of tickets, make sure to check with your theater for discount nights. On their least busy night many theaters offer discounted ticket prices to draw in more attendees. This can be a great way to enjoy a night at the theater while still staying on a budget.

Another idea is to look for second run movie theaters in your area. These theaters show films that have just finished their major theatrical run, and because of that the prices are deeply discounted. This is also a great way for you to catch that movie he or she wanted to see but you were never able to make it to!

Parks and community organizations often play classic films for free, and you can bring your own popcorn! Enjoy the nostalgia of the black and white films from the golden days of cinema, with their cheesy pickup lines and overly dramatic plots and acting. Outdoor showings at parks are also a nice change of pace as you sit under the stars on a blanket and listen to the sounds of the night play behind the celluloid love stories on the screen.

❀ Dog Park ❀

From Dalmatians to Dachshunds, Pugs to Poodles, the dog park is a carefree and relaxing location for your date with your partner (and your furry friends!). If you or your date has a dog, daily walks are part of the care and routine of your relationship with your pet and including your date in that routine can be a special time of bonding for all of you. Introduce your best friend to your special friend.

Enjoying an afternoon stroll down to the park gives you a time to chat and connect with your partner as you simply take in the day around you. Nothing beats the iconography of two lovers and their canine companions spending time together. It really is a true form of family and there is a peacefulness to that time.

Once you get to the dog park though, get ready for some playtime! Regardless of whether it's throwing a frisbee, a tennis ball, or playing tug of war with your dog, get your date involved and having fun as well. Dogs always seem to have endless energy so having someone there to take over for you when your arm tires of frisbee throwing might be an added benefit.

If your park allows it and your dog is trained well enough let them off the leash for a while and find a bench for you and your date to spend some quality time together. Grab a cup of coffee or tea from a nearby shop and slow down to enjoy nature and each other. Dogs are happy with the simple things: a little bit of room to run and a stick or ball to play with. Let your date know you appreciate the simple things as well, like just spending the afternoon at the park together.

❀ Duck Feeding ❀

Spend a quiet and relaxing afternoon with your date down at your local park. Bring along some treats for the local waterfowl and spend some time feeding the ducks together. As they migrate around you there might even be some ducklings for you to catch sight of!

Stay away from the traditional loaf of bread as it is unhealthy for the ducks. Instead, bring some rice, vegetable peels, or frozen peas with you to spread out for them. Nothing is quite as enchanting as watching all the birds come up onto the shore to peck and feed, stomping around in their webbed feet.

Bring some human snacks as well and sit back for a quick bite yourselves as you watch the waterfowl hunt and peck after the treats you left them. Nickname them together. See which ducks group together into little families with a mother, father, and ducklings and toss them a few extra treats. Also be on the lookout for geese and swans that might be nearby and will want in on the feast. Just be careful to keep a safe distance from these large and territorial waterfowl.

A simple, quiet afternoon feeding the ducks and holding your date's hand by the water can be all that you need for a memorable and romantic time together.

❀ Easter Egg Hunt w/Lover's Coupons ❀

Easter isn't at the top of the list of most romantic holidays, but you can add a little spice and sexiness to your next Easter with your lover with a simple game. Invite them to an Easter egg hunt, with plastic eggs filled with lover's "coupons."

Keep it simple. A coupon for a kiss or holding hands might set the tone for your romantic egg hunt. Or, depending on your partner, maybe they would be more enticed by the promise of a night out at their favorite restaurant or bar. Anything you can think of that your lover would enjoy can work, this is the perfect opportunity for you to demonstrate how much you know about them and what turns them on.

Intersperse small gifts with the coupons. Perhaps a piece of chocolate, a new bracelet or a set of earrings, or maybe tickets to their favorite show. These changes of pace will keep things interesting and keep your date guessing as well.

Use themes throughout your hunt. In the kitchen hide an egg with a coupon for making them dinner one night. Offer a sexy home video of yourself on a flash drive, and hide it behind the TV. An egg with a coupon for a night of passion might be tucked under the pillows in the bedroom. Just remember your partner can cash these any at any time so don't be surprised if you are expected to deliver on your promises then and there!

❋ Fast & Fabulous ❋

Are you and your darling in the mood for a gourmet meal, without the gourmet price? Is he (or she) not afraid of getting a little bit creative and trying something unusual? Then plan out a fast and fabulous candlelight dinner!

Not as intimidating as it sounds, this dinner is quite easy to put together! It all comes down to the details. Choose a table near the back of the restaurant, and arrive at a quiet time of night. Drape a wine red tablecloth on the table. Set your most elegant china, your classiest wine glasses, and your polished silverware in a fine dining layout. Fold your napkins, and lay your crisp white masterpieces on you and your date's seats.

Ask your date to come to a location down the street. Tell them to dress to the nines! Then, ask them to close their eyes (or bring a blindfold!) and walk them down the street to the establishment of your choice.

They will definitely be surprised and touched by your thoughtfulness and creativity when they see the spread that you have set out for them. For an elegant touch, bring some nonflammable candles to decorate the table, and give your date a beautiful flower (or bouquet!) to put in a vase you have brought.

Then comes the easy part — ordering dinner! Simply walk up to the counter, order your food, and it will be ready within minutes. Fill up your drinks, have a seat, and eat your burgers and fries in style. Don't forget the dessert! Now who is to say that convenient fare can't also be classy?

✳ Favorite Movie Night ✳

One of the best ways you can show your partner that you care about their interests and passions is to throw a favorite movie night for them. Whether it's an action flick, a romance, or a legal drama, showing a genuine interest in their favorite movie and by extension them is a great way to express how much you care for them.

Dim the lights, pop some popcorn, and turn off your phones (or at least turn off the ring tone). Make sure it is clear that this is a night to focus on a good film and spending time together, not being distracted by work, friends, or other obligations. Do some online research for great trivia questions about the film and make a short game about it. Everyone loves a good pop-quiz, right?

One of the advantages of movie night in your home is you can bring back the old school tradition of an intermission. A halfway stopping point through the film is a great way to introduce a new special snack you prepared, make a new cocktail, or just take a moment to stretch and talk about the film so far. Since it's their favorite film they will have a lot of great insight on the characters and themes. Ask them their analysis on it; let them be a movie critic for a few minutes.

As a follow up to your favorite movie night, find a piece of memorabilia from the film. Maybe a theater poster, the soundtrack, or a replica prop from the film and give that to them as a gift at the next birthday or holiday. This is a great way to tie themes throughout your relationship and reminisce about some of your favorite dates together. And a great perk is once you've thrown a favorite movie night for them, they will probably want to do the same for you.

❈ Game Show Taping ❈

Get ready for you and your date to come on down! You're the next contestant for a date at a live game show taping! If you're ready to get caught up in excitement, competition, and the chance to turn your luck around a live game show taping is a perfect date for you and your partner.

Participating in the audience of a live game show is a fun and unique experience. Tickets are free, just make sure you get on the waiting list with enough time in advance. If you are making a trip to another city where they are taping there usually is a better chance of getting in the audience than if you are applying for tickets in your home town.

Television offers many games shows, from Let's Make a Deal, Family Feud, The American Bible Challenge, Whose Line is it Anyway? improv to the audience driven The Price is Right. Get onto the right show and you might even have the opportunity to be a contestant pulled from the audience! But even if you spend the whole show in the seats, participation is key whether you're shouting out suggestions for contestants or cheering on your favorite competitor in a head to head battle.

Game shows are often taped ahead of time and then played during their TV time slot. Going to the taping then catching the broadcast on TV later is super fun, especially as you look for yourselves in the audience and relive the competitions together. It's always a great time when you and your date can take part in a classic American tradition.

✳ Happy Hour with Appetizers ✳

Don't let a hungry and grumbling stomach ruin your next night out with your date. Pop over to your favorite bar or restaurant for happy hour. In addition to drink specials, appetizers are normally half off and you can both get your fill while sampling a variety of tasty starters.

From spinach dip to chicken wings most bars and restaurants offer a great assortment of starters from which to choose. Chow down on soft pretzels, cheesy mozzarella sticks or get your cheeseburgers in miniature fashion with a plate of sliders. A couple plates of different appetizers is usually more than enough to satisfy a sudden craving or even the dinner hunger pangs, and you'll save a good chunk of change as well!

Can you say drink specials galore? $2 beers, half off margaritas, or maybe even some tasty Jell-O shots are all happy hour offerings that can infuse some fun and zest into any night out on the town. If you are out on a double date, take turns buying the rounds and treating everyone to a different drinks each time, variety is the spice of life and of your night out!

Both frugal and fun, an evening out at happy hour can be a great impromptu rendezvous with your date for a quick bite or the start to a wonderful evening full of adventures together. Make sure to follow up with a romantic walk through the city or a stopover at his or her favorite club for dancing and more drinks. It's always a good night to be in love and with the one you love.

❄ High School Sporting Event ❄

Get ready to paint your face and show some school spirit. For a raucous good time spend your next date taking in a high school sports game. From the hard hitting action of football to the squeaking of sneakers and leather against the hardwood basketball court, high school sports are exciting, high energy, and always fun.

If your date is local, visit their alma mater to cheer on the home-town team. Participate in raffles and drawings and grab a soft pretzel or popcorn to share. Learn the fight songs and scream along. If there is a pep band make sure to get to the game early to get into the spirit and get amped up for a night of intense competition.

During halftime tour the building and hear the stories your date has to tell of their high school days. Whether it's their first kiss under the stairs or flunking a math midterm there are plenty of nostalgic memories for you both to laugh and reminisce about together. Learning more about your partner's past will better help you understand and love them in the present.

No matter the outcome, make sure to stick around to the end of the game and cheer on the kids as they come off the field or court. Take a walk with your date to end the night and talk more about their high school glory days. And make sure to come back to support the team again, as high school sports are a proud tradition and a great outing for you and your partner to have a good time.

❈ Hiking Excursion ❈

Hiking is a fun, health conscious way to spend a day together with your date. Getting out and exploring nature together taking in majestic views and a quiet sunset will make the perfect date for you and your partner.

Be sure to meet up before hitting the trail to pack a small backpack with what you'll need for the day. Packed lunches, plenty of water, sunscreen and bug spray are a few of the necessities. Also pack a camera, a hiking map, and a first aid kit (just in case!).

Strike out on the trail early enough in the day that you have time to make a good trek and get back before sunset. Choose a trail with picturesque views and good stopping points. Whether that's a secluded waterfall or a majestic open view of the horizon, these stopping points are great photo ops and a welcome chance to rest before the next leg of the hike.

If there is a good view not far from your car, make sure to stop and take in the glowing sunset at the end of the day. Surprise him or her with a small bottle of wine you stowed away in the backpack, and enjoy a drink while sitting quietly watching the day end. Nothing is more romantic than enjoying the simple pleasures of nature together.

❈ Horseback Ride ❈

Horseback riding is something you and your date can both learn and enjoy together. It doesn't matter if you are brand new and need to learn the basics of riding or an experienced horseman, this age old tradition and pastime is a great way for you and your partner to bond together as you bond with your steed.

For the casual horseback rider, look for guided trail rides where you can be taken on a tour of local trails while having some expert supervision to make sure you can get any riding tips you need. Enjoy a throwback travel experience on these trails enjoying woodland nature scenes and the gentle pace of the horse below you. With a few quick tips and tricks you and your date will be enjoying a leisurely horseback ride and communing with nature.

If you are more serious about learning to ride or have some experience, taking lessons can be a great way to spend quality time together with your date learning a new skill. Equestrianism is an intricate and time honored sport that will challenge you both and build on a strong common interest. Smaller lesson settings will help you learn at your own pace together, so see if you can book lesson time together with one instructor. Participating together as you learn to trot, canter, and gallop with your horses will make learning all the more memorable.

❀ Horticulture Class ❀

Taking a horticulture class with your partner can be a great way to cultivate not just new flowers and plants, but your relationship as well. Working together to nurture and grow new life even in just the simple form of a daisy or tulip is a bond building experience that will draw you and your partner together. Sign up for a beginner's course to spend quality time with your date and learn some interesting and useful skills as well!

From the basics of gardening all the way to advanced pruning and splicing techniques a horticulture class offers a vast wealth of knowledge to learn. Get ready to dig your hands in the dirt and the mud as you till your plot, plant, and water seeds. Not only is it a great way to educate yourself but also to get outside and enjoy the sunshine. You need it as much as your plants do!

Turn gardening into an elongated exercise. Make plans with your date to go back together to check on your progress often. Make it a special time where you rendezvous even in the middle of a busy day to stop and tend to your garden together.

It's an age old analogy, but tending to your garden is much like tending to a relationship. It takes time, careful attention, and commitment. As you learn through your classes the best horticultural practices to grow a vibrant garden, be mindful of how some of those same principles can apply to your love life as well. Welcome Mother Nature's wisdom.

❀ Kayaking ❀

Paddle down the river at an easy pace or traverse rapids and small waterfalls with your partner on your next date. Kayaking is an adrenaline rush inducing activity that will have you and your partner amped up about spending time together. Nothing beats a day exploring the river!

Depending on your goal for the day there are a couple different types of kayaks to check out. If you are planning on hitting some whitewater, using traditional kayaks where you both have your own single seat boat is the best option as it provides the most maneuverability. If you are just looking for a way to cruise down a docile river together for the day consider a twin seat kayak where you both can work together to guide the boat and be close enough to still hold conversation during the trip.

Any water sport is about communication and teamwork. Whether you are working in tandem on a twin seat kayak or calling out rocks and currents to each other as you take separate boats down the whitewater, a day on the water will teach you how to better communicate together and build trust. A little hazardous white-water just might be what draws you two closer together!

Most kayaks have a place where you can stash a small bag so pack a lunch and stop off on the riverbank to enjoy a moment of rest with your partner. Take in the beauty of the water from the solid ground and just enjoy the sights and sounds for a moment with your date. Kayaking is a good workout and hard work, it's nice to take a moment to relax and connect with your date before heading back out into the currents.

❈ Living Escape ❈

Dreaming of sandy beaches and mojitos while the sounds of the ocean lull you to sleep? Or maybe trekking through the grasslands trying to catch an elusive view of a lion while on safari?

Chances are you can't pick up and go on vacation right this minute, but with a little imagination and ingenuity you and your date can spend the evening getting into the spirit of adventure by redesigning your living quarters to echo your favorite vacation destination.

The first step is visualizing your dreamy escape. Grab a pad of paper and itemize every detail of your date, writing down anything and everything. Brainstorm, brainstorm, brainstorm, and create! Find a computer and do some web searches to find images of rooms that might be similarly decorated to what you are imagining for inspiration. Look up details from the culture of where you want to visit for ideas of what to incorporate.

The next step—shopping. Hobby and home improvement stores will have all sorts of decorations and knick knacks at a reasonable price. Depending on your theme don't be afraid

geeky competition while you soak up the atmosphere of the phenomenon that is arcade gaming.

Arcade games come in all forms and there is sure to be something you both will love. From drift racing games that seat you and your date side by side in high octane competition to zombie shooting games that require you to work as a team to make sure you both make it through the apocalypse alive, arcades are a great way to have fun in tandem. Grab a joystick and battle it out on Street Fighter or work your way together past classic super villains in Captain America and the Avengers.

Taking a step back into the golden age of gaming, try out retro machines like PacMan and Frogger. Switch things up from the digital to the analog and challenge your date to a game of Pinball. Not only are these gaming classics nostalgic and a good conversation starter, they have stood the test of time and are a blast to play!

And if you or your date is a diehard gamer you can continue the fun at home with arcade cabinet rentals. For a monthly fee you can have a different arcade cabinet shipped to your home every month for you and your partner to enjoy whenever the mood strikes. Who knows, it might just spark some friendly competition for that high score. And if you're spending time playing with your date, everyone wins.

❄ Local Fitness Center (Gymnasium) ❄

Closing time for the gym is fast approaching. The lights are low outside and most people have finished their workouts and headed home leaving a calm silence through the building. Bring your date at twilight to take advantage of the empty facilities and enjoy the jacuzzi and sauna together.

Don't worry about working out beforehand, just come to relax and unwind together. Slip into the jacuzzi and sit close together, letting the water move over you both and slowly work out some of the day's kinks and knots from your muscles. Talk through the day's challenges and triumphs, letting your minds relax and destress as well. There shouldn't be a care in the world other than each other.

Follow up the jacuzzi with a visit to the sauna together. The sizzle of the steam rising off the coals and the smell of the saturated wood grain should ease you as you let your skin detox and soften. Lie back and let your eyes close, quietly melting in the humidity. Don't feel obligated to stay longer than you are comfortable, the best is yet to come.

Find out if your gym offers couples massage. Step into the massage room to low lights and soothing background music, greeted by the warm and calming presence of your masseuses. Settle into the tables and let the last of your cares and thoughts from the day fall away from you as you are kneaded and molded by the skilled hands of your masseuse into heaven. If you are close enough, holding your lover's hand during the massage can express your mutual bliss.

After your massages, take a moment to sit alone in the room with your lover. It will take some advanced planning, but have a bowl of fresh fruit nearby (his or her favorite kind) that you can both enjoy. Stimulate all the senses by feeding them large juicy strawberries or plump and bursting red grapes. It is the perfect flourish to a sensual and romantic evening together you won't soon forget.

✿ Local Theatre Plays/ Musicals ✿

You don't have to live in New York City to appreciate good theater. Check out your local theater for seasonal plays and musicals put on by talent that is working right in your backyard.

From classic musicals like Annie to new age classics like The Rocky Horror Picture Show a local or community theater caters to all sorts of tastes and genres. Relive your childhood together at a showing of Peter Pan or experience the sober and experimental simplicity of Our Town. Supporting your local theater not only furthers the arts and artists, but gives you a chance to sample live performances you never would have seen if you hadn't looked past Broadway.

Apart from traditional plays, look for originally written material by local writers that is being performed. While it's true not every work will be a sensation, many gems of the theater can go unnoticed and finding those by proactively attending local theater can be a rewarding experience for you both. And if you or your partner is theatrically inclined, consider getting involved in a production. Working together to memorize lines, practice blocking, and rehearse with the rest of the cast gives you just another excuse to spend time together and fall deeper in love.

✿ Lover's Scavenger Hunt ✿

For a tantalizing, sensual, and fun evening together you and your date can participate in a scavenger hunt. Leave behind clues, and riddles...decide on twist prior to activity.

Prep the scavenger hunt by assembling both your items and taking turns scattering and hiding them in different parts of the house. Then present your date with a list of what you've hidden and see how many they can find...and how many you lose! Get creative with your hiding a spot, the longer the game draws out the more scintillating each new find becomes.

You may start to lose your shirt, socks, and belt; make sure to keep things interesting by taking breaks to compare notes and maybe get a hint or two from your partner. It shouldn't be too simple to find your date's items, but too difficult can spoil the fun of the game as well. It's perfectly fine to help out if needed.

No matter how intimate you and your partner are this can still be a great game. If you are just starting dating bundle up and play to see who loses their jacket, hat and socks first. If you and your lover are more intimate, take it all the way and see who ends up au naturale. It can be as silly and innocent or as sexy and tempting as you want it to be.

❀ Martial Arts Movie Night ❀

The anxiously awaiting student wipes clammy hands over the sweat from his brow. His master stands before him, a challenging pillar of strength and battle tested skill. The student makes a fist, the sinews of his arm tightening up to his shoulder. With a swift motion he strikes, letting out a loud "Hi-Yaaa!" Ok, chances are he's a lot more into this scenario than she is. But a good martial arts movie can be a fun escape from the cares and worries of the real world and a great way to treat him on your next date.

From Jet Li's Fist of Legend to The Matrix and The Man with the Iron Fists martial arts movies are extreme, loud, spectacular, and an all-around good time. If there isn't a new kung fu film playing in theaters, a quick Google search turns up several "top 10" lists for martial arts movies. Pick one or two classics and let him know to prepare himself for a night of board breaking, bone crunching, gravity defying action.

An Asian theme evening is perfect for the atmosphere. Soft Oriental music in the background, low candlelight, and cushions on the floor for chairs will put him in the mood for adventures in distant lands. Chinese takeout is perfectly acceptable but if you are so inclined cook up a fresh Oriental dish of your own to really put the magic touch on things.

Once the movie starts, make sure to get into it as much as he does. If a character makes a particularly devastating attack, yell along with your guy and let him know you're enjoying the over the top action as well. The other option is to choose a particularly awful film on purpose and enjoy mocking the cheesy action and dialogue together. Deadly and death defying can also be fun!

At the end of the night make sure to have a memento of the evening, whether that's a DVD of an old and hard to find kung fu flick, a decorative pair of chopsticks, or karate belt of his own. Having something to take away from the evening and reminisce about it will encourage a sequel in the near future!

❋ Neighborhood Zoo ❋

"Lions and tigers and bears. Oh my!" While you probably don't have to worry about houses falling from the sky and wicked witches chasing after you and your dog, a day at the zoo does provide a great way to experience lions, tigers, bears and many more exotic creatures with your lover. Spending the day outside taking in the most beautiful and bizarre of nature's creatures is a fun and playful date you both will enjoy.

The best part about a day at the zoo is it offers probably the most variety of any activity in which you and your date can participate. In addition to the vast array of different animals, birds, and insects many zoos have shows where you can watch dolphins perform acrobatics or elephants paint works of art. Petting zoos allow you to get closer to some of the more gentle creatures (or the not so gentle, as in the case of a shark touching tank!).

For a slightly more intimate setting, see if your zoo has a botanical or bamboo garden and spend some time quietly walking, holding hands, and talking. Try to schedule this in the middle of your trip to the zoo to give you both some much needed rest from trying to get to every exhibit you can and just enjoy the serenity and beauty of nature's flora.

The insect and reptile section may not be everyone's favorite but there are hundreds of fascinating species to see here and learn about. Who knows, your date might just surprise you and have more of an affinity for nature's misunderstood creatures than you expected.

A fun activity you can try is a zoo scavenger hunt. Make a list of different animals and species and challenge your date to a race to see who can find them all first. Log all the animals you've visited with photos on your phone and send them a picture update to keep the competition interesting each time you find your next animal. The loser has to wear a children's animal mask for the rest of the day!

❉ Paddle Boats ❉

Spend the day relaxing on the lake just off the shore with your date, slowly maneuvering through the water and taking in the sunshine together in a paddleboat. Paddleboats are one of the safest and most laid back ways to spend a day on the water, so if you are looking for a change of scenery and a quiet getaway this could be the perfect water transport for you.

There is little danger of tipping over in a paddleboat, so long as you don't mind your feet getting a bit damp you shouldn't have to worry about bringing a towel or change of clothes on this outing. Pack a few snacks and drinks, and bring along a camera to take pictures of the view and the two of you having a good time.

Paddleboats require both passengers to work together pedaling the boat so you and your date can have fun working on getting in sync to take turns in the boat. Pedal hard to get to the middle of the lake and then just relax, floating lazily and soaking up the sun. You can spend all day on the water in a paddleboat. Stash a pack of cards away in your bag for an appropriate game of Go Fish out on the water, or bring along poles and actually go fishing for the day together.

As the current slowly pulls you back to shore you can backpedal slowly and keep you both out on the water a little longer. There's no rush to go anywhere, just being on the water holding your date's hand and letting the lap of the waves lull you both into relaxation makes for an ideal afternoon. A paddleboat is the perfect lover's transport, built for two and specifically designed for leisure.

❊ Photo with Easter Bunny ❊

It's Easter and everyone in town is out on an Easter egg hunt. Take your date out and enjoy the festivities and the family fun together by joining in the joyful celebration of spring and new life. Sign up for a local egg hunt to participate in the festivities!

Spending the morning in the park hunting for eggs, helping children find hidden treasures, and enjoying the vibe and family atmosphere can be a great low-key way to spend time with your date. Go all out by wearing matching spring sweaters and embracing the cheesy photo opportunities. Be on the lookout for the Easter Bunny who will be there to greet the children, a photo op with him shouldn't be missed! Save the snapshot as part of your joint remembrances of times you've spent together.

No matter your belief system, Easter is a time to celebrate new life, new opportunities and fresh start. What better time for a budding romance or a rekindling of passion? And what better way to embrace those opportunities than you and your partner finding your inner child again and enjoying Easter like children do; with wide eyed rapture at the colors, sights, sounds, and that magical giant bunny you have photographic proof exists :)

❀ Photo with Santa ❀

It's just a few days before Christmas and you and your date are out shopping at the mall getting those last minute gifts. The banisters and rafters are strung with garland and lights, the PA system croons classic Christmas songs and it's just a great time to be in love. Like most malls, this one has a North Pole station where kids can get a picture with Santa Claus. Don't let the fact that you are mature adults discourage you, step into the line and get your own picture with St. Nick this holiday season!

Wish Santa a Merry Christmas and make sure to thank him for being there for all the kids. Get a picture with the three of you and make sure to pick up the prints from the photographer. Then, head over to the nearest gift store and pick out a frame for the photo together. Take your time finding the perfect one, this will be a holiday keepsake for both of you for years to come. Set the photo over your mantel for Christmas morning as you open gifts together to remind you about your fun encounter with Santa.

Send the photo out to your family and friends on social media and let them know about the good times you are having as well. The holidays are a time for sharing love and good cheer with one another, and nothing does that better than the childlike spirit and joy of Santa Claus.

❄ Pizza n' $2 Buck Chuck ❄

The evening is starting to fall over the city and you and your partner are out for a date. If you aren't feeling the formal vibe of going out to dinner, create your own gourmet restaurant on the harbor as you watch the sunset and the ships. Easier than you'd imagined without breaking the bank!

Stop off at a pizzeria on your way to the docks and pick up a flatbread pizza to share. It shouldn't be more than about $8 and paired with a bottle of $2 Chuck (Charles Shaw brand wine) you will be enjoying fine dining by the water in no time and for about ten dollars.

Watch the last of the ships roll into the harbor as you enjoy the warm flavorful pizza and sip wine together. The quiet lulling sound of the waves against the docks and the peaceful dimming of the sunset lights are better than any candlelight restaurant with music playing overhead. Allow Mother Nature to set the stage for this perfect evening.

Toast each other and your ingenuity in creating your own dining tradition. Kick off your shoes and enjoy the feel of the water against your toes, quietly holding hands and watching the sun go down on another day. Tomorrow is filled with promises and more wonderful times spent together.

✹ Pottery Class ✹

Of all the different arts you and your date can participate in together, pottery is one of the most challenging, rewarding, and sensual. Take a pottery class with your lover and practice the art of creation together as you mold the clay and express your creativity.

Take your time, patience is key when shaping clay. Whether you are slipping and scoring to assemble geometric pieces or throwing clay on the wheel to press and mold a bowl or urn, it's important to develop a sensitive touch and a careful, patient eye. That same patience and careful attention is needed in a relationship as well, so let your one feed the other and learn to give tender attention to your lover as well.

Work together on a piece, sitting near each other and letting your hands intertwine as you shape the clay. Let this be a sensual experience for both of you, moving earth, water and each other to create something together. Don't be afraid of making a mess, the fun is in not caring about appearances and just focusing on each other.

After your piece has been shaped it's time to glaze and fire it. Make sure you initial this piece together in remembrance of this day. After it is fired in the kiln and finished you can display it proudly in your home, a token of a beautiful time spent with your lover.

✹ Rock Climbing ✹

Rain or shine, winter or summer you and your date can go on a rock climbing adventure just by visiting your local gym. Call ahead and find out what gyms offer climbing walls, often they will offer free time slots where families and enthusiasts can come and enjoy the fun. This is a great way for you and your date to have a good time while staying frugal!

Dress properly. Sturdy sneakers, shorts, and close fitting t-shirts or tank tops that won't catch on anything are a must. Get in the spirit by purchasing climbing shoes that fit your feet snugly and help you grip the rocks with your toes. Grab a couple of water bottles and you're ready to head out.

Once you're at the wall it's time to get hooked up into the harness, dust some chalk on your hands, and get climbing! Make sure to cheer on your date as they scale the wall. If you can both climb at once, make sure to help each other out by suggesting nearby handholds and offering encouragement. Don't get ahead of your date by too much. Reaching the top together will prompt a celebratory high five!

If you both feel confident with the standard walls see if there is an advanced section, with less handholds and angled portions to climb up and under. Challenge yourselves so the victory is that much sweeter. But whether you are able to conquer the advanced walls or not, make sure to end the day on a positive note taking stock of your climbing accomplishments together.

✹ Rock Exploration ✹

For the geology lovers out there, spend your next date exploring and educating yourselves on your local geological features with a rock exploration. Round out your adventure with a scavenger hunt and a picnic lunch; who knew rocks could be so romantic?!

Most of us as children had a rock collection at one time or another. Anything from pebbles to semi-precious stones might have made it into our collection pails and plastic divider cases. With the vast wealth of geological knowledge now available through a simple web search it's easy to take that hobby to the next level and share that passion for finding rare pieces with your date. Do some research on what stones are indigenous to your locale, and then build a list for you to check off together as you hike. Remember the license plate game? Well it's sort of like that.

Make sure to stop along the way to take in the beauty of the rocks you find around you. Whether it's the textured and finely layered beauty of sandstone, the glowing appeal of quartz, or the inky blackness of obsidian a closer look will reveal that the rocks we walk by without a thought every day contain more wonder than we ever imagined. This simple discovery together can be a wonderful moment of bonding for you and your date.

And any adventure outdoors calls for a picnic lunch. Lay out your treasures on the picnic blanket and compare lists, seeing who has found more items. Hold that piece of quartz up to the sun and see how the light softly filters through it. Remind your date that they are the most precious of gems to you, more beautiful than anything you might find of the beaten path.

❈ Salsa Dancing ❈

Get ready to spice up your love life with a bit of Latino culture by signing up for Salsa dancing classes! Let your hips do the talking with your partner and learn a fun and sexy new dance step that will have you both passionate about dance and about each other.

Salsa classes are a great way to loosen up and enjoy the fun spirit of dance. The emphasis is all on movement and rhythm, and the freeform nature of the dance allows you both to express yourselves creatively too. Make sure to pay attention to your partner and get in tune with their movements, remembering to go with the flow and let the music carry you both someplace special.

After taking a few classes, head out on the town and check out a salsa dance exhibition. Watching the professionals can be a bit daunting but it's an impressive and sexually charged display that is thrilling to watch and something to aspire to in your own dance. Knowing a bit about how the technique and steps should be will help you better appreciate the skill and expertise these pros show in their displays.

Definitely take time to practice your moves at home with each other, honing your steps, spins, and flourishes. The initial steps may be easy to pick up, but there are an infinite number of combinations and variations to try with each other. It's a fun activity that you both can enjoy all through your relationship.

❄ Scenic Walking Tour (San Francisco) ❄

Whether you're a local or just visiting, San Francisco is a beautiful bay city with numerous historical and artistic sites to see. Plan your next date around a day full of seeing all San Francisco has to offer.

Start with the Golden Gate Bridge. This landmark of San Francisco has a rich history and is an awesome thing to behold in person. Strike out on foot or bicycle to avoid the tolls and take in the view of the bay and the San Francisco skyline. Going with a tour bus will open up your mind to some of the history of its construction and the tragic and triumphant stories of the men who built it.

The next golden item on our list is Golden Gate Park. This tranquil and exotic park features flower conservations, botanical gardens, and the Japanese Tea Garden where you can walk intimately around traditional Japanese architecture and bamboo forests. From redwood trees to grazing bison, the Golden Gate Park is a wonder to see.

Alcatraz is your next stop! This legendary prison provides a great guided tour where you can see the holding place of some of the hardest criminals of the 20th century. Make sure to plan well in advance for this tour, as it's often sold out. Learn about the infamous 1962 escape from Alcatraz, and see the cell of legendary mobster Al Capone. This thrilling and historical tour is a great way to have an adventure together without worrying about ending up in the slammer!

End your day with a barefoot stroll in the sand taking in the ocean view. San Francisco's beauty speaks volumes. Take a cable car to Fisherman's Wharf and watch the boats come in from the day. Cutting over to Pier 39 you'll find nighttime dining and entertainment to cap off the day. Your day barely scratched the surface of all there is to see and do in the city, plan another one soon!

❀ Sewing Class ❀

Whether you just need to learn how to mend a shirt, sew back on a button, or want to make a quilt for around the house, a sewing class is a practical and fun way to spend time with your significant other.

If you don't see a sewing class advertised at your local art center, Jo-Ann fabric and craft stores often hold classes and can be found across the country. They also offer buy one class get one class free specials so you can plan two dates and see how much progress you've made.

Working on a project in your sewing class together can be a fun bonding experience. Make a throw pillow that will be shared in your living room, or craft gifts for each other. Everyone can use a tote! Ladies, if you are more advanced than he is encourage him as he tries his hand at a traditionally feminine skill. Gentlemen, appreciate the nimbleness and precision it takes her to simply get a button back onto a shirt!

Coming away from a class with a good life skill and some fun opportunities to do crafts together is a worthwhile date in any relationship. Building a relationship is about shared experiences and making memories, and learning how to sew together will give you that for years to come!

❄ Snow Play Date ❄

You wake up from a long night's sleep, pull open the curtains and overnight the world has been transformed into a winter wonderland by the season's first snowfall. Take full advantage of the fresh coat of white by scheduling a "playdate" in the snow with your lover.

If you don't have a yard at your home meet them at the park and make sure to bring along some necessary tools. For snowman building you'll need a carrot, some pieces of coal or large black buttons, a hat, scarf, and a corncob pipe. Just make sure they bring the same! Challenge your date to a snowman building contest where the winner gets to pick the next date location and activity. Go big or go home! Build your snowman as large as you can so you have the best chance of choosing that next special date.

Build a snowman, and customize this experience especially for your date. Arrange snow angels in unorthodox patterns. Finish with two angels next to each other, close enough that you can lie and hold hands at the end, watching the snow drift down lazily from the sky.

Don't worry if a friendly snowball fight breaks out, while you were building your snowman you secretly built a stash of snowballs behind him! Duck for cover and try to rapid fire at your date until they surrender. Demand a kiss in payment for the war, it's a tribute they won't mind surrendering.

Before you leave your date get photos of you with your snowmen to print and frame on your wall. And get ready for the next snowfall, where another date in the snow is sure to be a hit.

❄ Summer Concert Series (FREE) ❄

From jazz festivals, to college choruses, to live music in the park, nothing promises a good time like a summertime concert series. A concert can be a great way to break the ice on a first date, or rekindle that spark of romance and passion you've been looking for. Good music can draw people together and help build shared experiences and memories that last for a lifetime.

For that first date, live music in the park might be the perfect way to learn more about your significant other's taste and personality. Open-air venues often book nightly music from local artists, and having the opportunity to discover a new favorite musician together is both exciting and a great way to begin building a relationship based on shared interests.

For a more formal date setting, look into concerts by local orchestras, small operas, and colleges that put on summertime performances. Taking in a bit of higher culture is a great way for you and your date to be stimulated intellectually and emotionally. It may be intimidating going to a formal setting on a first date (or even a second or third!), but take it as an opportunity to look your best and show off for your special someone. Bringing flowers or a gift for your partner is completely appropriate and a great way to show you thought about them and went the extra mile.

A jazz concert, with its improvisational nature and smooth sounds, can be a great way to set the mood for a night of romance. Suit up, Gents! Ladies, slip into that little black dress you save for special occasions. Nothing says classy and sexy like a night at the jazz club. Coupled with drinks and finding a cozy spot to enjoy the show, an evening of jazz is the perfect way to rekindle romance and passion.

Finding that special band, orchestra, or singer/songwriter that you both love to listen to is a fun and engaging way to spend the summer with your date. Sharing an evening of good music together can be a building block in growing a relationship and an experience you'll want to repeat for years to come.

❈ Sunset at the Marina ❈

Take a few hours to stop by the marina with your date tonight and watch the sunset come down over the water. Bring along a bottle of wine or a couple of beers and just enjoy the cool breeze off the water as the sky turns orange and purple. A relaxing night of conversation and nature's beauty is yours for the taking.

Watch the last ships of the day pull in, slowly trekking home from long days full of ocean adventures. Talk about what they might have been doing out on the water all day, maybe fishing or racing or just navigating the waves with no cares at all. Talk about what adventures the two of you could have on the water and make plans for going out soon.

Take off your shoes and dip your feet in the ocean letting the saltwater massage and saturate you. After most of the sun has set and it's just starting to get dark you can walk barefoot back along the wooden decks of the marina and romanticize about the next time you will be out there for another sunset together. Letting the sun fall to your back with the sounds of the ocean playing softly behind you is the perfect setting for a night of city adventures and romance.

❋ Swimming Class ❋

If you are looking to get in shape while spending time with your partner, signing up for swimming classes for your next date could be the perfect option. Whether you can only doggy paddle or are proficient in the butterfly and backstroke enjoying time together in the pool while getting tips on your swimming prowess is a great way to stay healthy and spend time together.

Swimming is a great way to exercise. The combination of a strong cardio workout and the low impact nature of working out in the water creates an ideal environment for getting into shape without killing your joints. Adult swim classes vary in complexity. Sign up for the most basic of courses if you've never learned to swim, or if you want to work on your diving techniques you can try out an advanced class. Make sure your date is comfortable with whatever level you choose, it's about having fun!

Synchronized swimming is also something covered in many adult swim classes, and this can be the perfect way for you to turn a lesson into a date. Working with your partner to move in harmony and practicing outside of class will promote a deeper bond between you, as you learn each other's timing and unspoken language. Being in sync with your partner is important in a relationship just like in synchronized swimming.

Eventually as you both become more proficient you can work to help improve each other's swim strokes and speed. Working together to swim a faster lap, or even racing each other in friendly competition is a great way to apply your lessons. Swim lessons are offered year-round so grab your suit and dive in with your date soon.

❀ Teach Him How to Bake a Cake ❀

There are a lot of great male chefs in the world, some of the finest restaurants in France, Italy, and America are helmed by them. But across the board men are notorious for this simple fact: they can't cook. Your man may be great at making a grilled cheese on an iron but teaching him how to bake could be a great way to spend time together and give him a much needed life lesson.

Step One: determine what you'd like to bake together. Find out what type of cake he likes the best and suggest you start with that. Make sure he helps with the whole process, from buying the ingredients with you at the store to washing dishes at the end. Make a point of making every part of the experience something fun. Washing dishes shouldn't be a chore, but the culmination of a great day spent together.

After you've bought all the ingredients take control of the situation by delegating yourself to "recipe reader." This makes sure that he does all the work and actually learns by doing, while still giving you the ability to supervise and make sure he uses the baking powder, not the baking soda.

Once the cake is in the oven and baking, show him how to maintain a clean kitchen by using the downtime to wash the dishes. Emphasize that the best part of enjoying what you've baked is not having to worry about the cleanup as you're eating.

Don't be afraid to get playful with the water, just be prepared to get splashed back!

Now that the cake is finished baking it's time to frost it. Demonstrate to him how to get a smooth, even layer of frosting on the cake, but don't worry if it turns into a challenge of how much frosting can fit on top. This is the creative part of the cake making and anything goes!

Everything is finished, the cake is frosted and the kitchen is clean. It's time to enjoy the fruits of your labor. Make sure to cut a slice while it's still warm and make sure to comment on the great job that he did. Just make sure he knows you expect him to surprise you with something tasty now that he knows how.

Volunteer at Neighborhood Shelter/Non-Profit Facility

Taking time to do things with your significant other that are fun and treating them is one of the joys of being in a relationship. But from time to time, it's good to remember those who are less fortunate than you are and to spend your time not on each other, but volunteering to help those in need. There are several non-profit facilities that are always looking for volunteers and this could be a great way for the two of you to participate in a cause that will help someone in need and enrich your own lives.

Check with your local homeless shelters and soup kitchens to see when they most need volunteers. It only takes a few hours of your time to go serve meals and interact with the needy, but you can have a tremendous impact on their day and their lives. Handing out clothes, hygiene kits, and meals will have a profound impact on how you both see the world around you and help you better empathize with people in hard situations.

Another organization to consider getting involved with is Habitat for Humanity. On the weekend you can pick up a hammer and a saw and help them build a home for a family that needs affordable living, drastically changing lives. Spending time together sweating and working to build something that lasts and will change a family's life is a rewarding and fulfilling experience, and a great way to extend the love you feel for each other beyond yourselves.

Whether you are donating time at a food bank, serving meals at a shelter, or hammering nails at a build site, it's important to take time to give back to the community and to those in need. It doesn't have to be a romantic date for it to be worthwhile of you and your partner's time; often giving is the best way to receive. Take time soon to spend the day with your partner working to make the world a better place.

❀ Wine Tasting ❀

Whether it's a crisp glass of Sauvignon Blanc or a rich and fruity Cabernet, a wine tasting has something for everyone and is a great way to try new experiences and tastes with your date. If you don't know much about wine and can't tell a Pinot Grigio from a Pinot Gris, don't worry! Most wine tastings are very well organized and there is always a sommelier (a professional knowledgeable about all things wine) around to help answer your questions.

Wine tastings come in many forms, from private clubs to vineyards open to the public. Keep an eye out for estates that have their own private vineyards, oftentimes they will hold wine tastings open to the public several times a year. Finding someplace local is a great way to spark conversation with your date and find points of connection.

If you are adventurous, plan a trip to wine country in Sonoma or Napa, California. Here you will find the best vineyards in America, and there are tastings and events all year long. A cute bed and breakfast, a leisurely day of sipping on different red and whites paired with fruits and cheese, and a quiet evening in the countryside is the perfect canvas for a budding romance.

When at the wine tasting, engage your date with questions about the different flavors and textures of the wine. Ask them to describe not just what they taste, but what they feel and what it reminds them of. Take the opportunity to learn more about their likes and dislikes not just with wine, but as a person. Wine tastings are the perfect way to enjoy the flavors of the season, while still cultivating and growing a new relationship.

❃ Yacht Dinner Cruise ❃

Sea salt, crisp breezes and an air of adventure. Boating is one of the best ways to spend the summer months and one of the best environments to spend time with your significant other. A yacht club offers all the fun and excitement of boating along with a vibrant social atmosphere.

Most yacht clubs are structured around a racing program. Here is a great opportunity for the spirit of competition to bring you and your date together, as you work together to claim victory. Bringing out the competitive nature in your partner can ignite sparks of passion and the teamwork necessary to sail a yacht is a perfect bonding experience.

If competition isn't your forte just take the afternoon to sail leisurely around the coast and enjoy the fresh air together.

Bring a packed lunch and bottle of wine and make plans to spend the whole day together away from the worries and stress of mainland life.

On the social side of things, a yacht club offers a great opportunity to meet likeminded people and enjoy a cocktail with good conversation. Meeting each other's friends and making new ones together builds strong common ground in the relationship and offers the chance for double dates, group outings, and other fun expeditions for you and your date in the future!

Whether it's high seas adventure and competition or a relaxing evening of dining and drinks with friends, a yacht club offers the perfect day for you and your date. Taking advantage of the warm summer weather to spend time on the water is a relaxing and stress-free excursion and something you will talk about for months and perhaps years to come.

❀ Zumba ❀

Zumba is an energetic and fast paced dance workout that will have you and your date moving to the Latin beats while secretly burning off calories and getting in shape! Sign up for a Zumba class at your local gym or dance studio and get ready to dance till you drop.

Zumba is all about losing yourself in the music and beats so you don't think about the workout you are getting. This is the perfect way to turn a workout into a date, you can both dance together and have a fun time for your daily workout! Classes range from standard dancing to using a chair as a prop or partner to aquatic Zumba. Try one, try them all! It's about having fun so make sure to take advantage of the variety.

This dance workout is something you can take home with you and practice anytime with your partner. Feeling a bit blue or lackadaisical? Turn up some music and start moving with your partner, before you know it you both will be in high spirits and high energy again! Zumba goes beyond just the workout, it is a lifestyle that incorporates music, culture, dance, and exercise. After a while you will find yourself permeated with the culture of the movement and that is a change that is healthy both for your body and your soul.

Attractions

🌺 Adventure Landing 🌺

Looking for some adventure on your next date? Visit Adventure Landing Amusement Park! With 18 parks to choose from and all admission-free, there is sure to be something for everyone. Play at the Mountain Magic Fun center in Ohio, or visit the Shipwreck Island Water Park in Jacksonville, Florida.

🌺 Adventure Park 🌺

Bring a date, or your family, to Adventure Park USA. Maryland's grandest pit stop for family entertainment, there is plenty to do and see here! Bumper cars, rock walls, laser tag, and a ropes course are only a few of the many activities. There is even a daycare so the adults can enjoy year round!

🌺 African Wildlife and Safari 🌺

Up close & Personal—Get ready for a wild time at the African Wildlife and Safari park! Your date will love choosing between the walking-thru or drive-thru safari. A close encounter with the Giraffes, Zebras, and Guanacos is guaranteed to be a memorable experience.

🌺 America's Stonehenge 🌺

Visiting England? Neither am I! But if you'd like to take your date to one of the oldest and well-known wonders of the world (well almost), America's Stonehenge may be the perfect place. Marvel at the Alpacas, and take advantage of snowshoeing activities. Don't forget to take your camera along to capture this marvelous adventure of a lifetime!

❋ Balboa Segway Tour ❋

Take your sweetheart on a unique tour—the Balboa Segway Tour! Listen as your professional tour guide explains the sites and historical markers, such as the Spanish Colonial Revival buildings. This is definitely a unique way to explore sunny Balboa Park. Reserve your tour today!

❋ Boardwalk Amusement Park ❋

Interested in visiting the world's best seaside amusement park? You and your date should love the Boardwalk Amusement Park! Walk the sandy shores of the Santa Cruz Beach. Enjoy roller coasters and carousels, while kissing the crisp ocean breeze! Santa Monica is my favorite.

❋ Buccaneer Bay Waterpark ❋

Buccaneer Bay Waterpark can be found in 26 of our 50 United States of America. Traveling through Lafayette, Indiana? Be sure that you and your sweetheart don't miss the Buccaneer Bay Waterpark! Tucked inside a Best Western hotel, this capacious place is the only indoor waterpark in Lafayette! With a monster slide, kiddie pool, hot tub and even an arcade, why not spend the entire day so you don't miss a thing!

✺ Cemetery After Hours ✺

Think "outside" the coffin with a cemetery tour after hours. This spooky event will make even the staunchest cynic a bit wary. Visit beautiful gothic headstones and intricately carved tombs. Hear the stories of how people have come to be here – you'll experience the normal, paranormal, and the unexpected!

✺ Conservation Center ✺

Is your date a lover, perhaps a collector of fine art? The conservation center may be the perfect place to visit. Inform yourselves of how fine art is restored and preserved. With paintings, sculptures, rare books and other artifacts, there is sure to be something for every art lover!

✺ Comedy Pet Theatres ✺

Do you and your sweetheart love the theatre? For a comical twist, treat them to a night at the Comedy Pet Theatre! Join Comedian Gregory Popovich's antics along with his adorable furry friends. All of the cats and dogs featured were rescued from animal shelters and trained by Mr. Popovich personally!

✺ Dinosaur Ridge ✺

If you and your date's travels take you out West, stop at the Dinosaur Ridge. Located in beautiful Colorado, you can literally walk where dinosaurs have been! Take a picture of dinosaur tracks and fossils. Discover where some of the world's most well-known dinosaur remains—Stegosaurus and Apatosaurus, among others were found.

✳ Empty Grave Haunted House Experience ✳

Are you and your date in the mood for a good scare? Then swing on by the Empty Grave Experience in Anaheim, California. With countless spooks, this haunted experience will definitely leave you petrified. From Grave Girls to a The Grave Cadillac Hearse, you are sure to get your share of thrills!

✳ French Quarter Phantoms ✳

Looking for a creepy good time? Then take your date to the French Quarter Phantoms! The ghouliest place in New Orleans, this knowledgeable ghost tour will give you the inside scoop about local New Orleans ghosts—and their stories. Sign up for the True Crime tour and Ghost and Vampire tour and learn about history in a whole new way!

✳ Ghost Tour ✳

If the paranormal sounds intriguing to you and your date, seek out a ghost tour. History exploration of these ghoulish tours will be a discussion for years to come. Visit exact locations people claim apparitions have been spotted. From haunted houses to graveyards there are plenty of paranormal tales to be told and sights to see!

❉ Harper Fowlkes House ❉

Georgia is known for more than peaches! On your next road trip down South, take your date to the Harper Fowlkes House! A rich and interesting heritage, this house has been handed down from generation to generation. Learn about its current place in history as home to the Society of the Cincinnati, an organization claiming to include descendants of George Washington's officers of the great Revolutionary War.

❉ Holocaust Memorial ❉

Are you waiting for an opportunity to delve into historic culture? Then take your darling to the Holocaust Memorial Center. The Holocaust Museum in Michigan is a major tourist attraction—this place is definitely a must-see. With an expansive Holocaust Center, as well as two museums, the Museum of European Jewish Heritage, and the International Institute of the Righteous, this promises to be an informative visit for religious and non-religious visitors alike.

❉ Illusions 308 ❉

Have you been craving trickery, stunts and illusions in your life? You and your date will love the Illusions 308 show in Las Vegas! This stunning conglomeration of magicians is sure to pique your interest, as well as make you wonder, "However did they do that?" Don't miss the magic!

❀ Joe Dumar's Fieldhouse ❀

Take your next date to the Joe Dumar's Fieldhouse. Founded by Joe Dumar, the great Detroit Pistons shooting guard, you can learn some sports history and get involved in fun activities as well. There is plenty to do and see! Try your hand at bungee trampolining, mini-lane bowling, or laser tag.

❀ Kennedy Tour ❀

Traveling along Boston's highway I-90 or I-93? You and your sweetheart will love the Kennedy Tour. Located in Cambridge, this guided tour is just over an hour and a half. Visits sites such as the JFK statue, Union Oyster House, and the beautiful Rose Kennedy Greenway. Enjoy learning about the highlights of Kennedy's rise to fame—from Congressman all the way to President of the United States.

❀ Lake Arrowhead Resort ❀

Looking for an exciting getaway? Arrowhead Resort might be just the place. There are plenty of activities to choose from, such as the Wildlife Sanctuary, sledding and skiing hills. Perfect for an all-day bonding experience with nature!

❀ Living Coast Discovery Center ❀

While visiting San Diego, take your date to the Living Coast Discovery Center. Curious how the San Diego Bay ecosystem works? Allow the

Living Coast Discovery Center staff to fill you in on all there is to know about its habitats. With sharks, turtles and plenty of scenic trails, there won't be a shortage of things to see and discover!

❋ Mission Beach Attractions ❋

Visiting the southwest United States? Take a detour to San Diego. While in San Diego, take your date to some of the beautiful Mission Beach attractions! Take a walk amidst nature at the Family Islands National Park, Paronella Park, and the Clump Mountain National Park. Then take to the ocean to see the Great Barrier Reef and to the ground for the 500-year old Cathedral Fig Tree. In addition to enjoying the sights, take advantage of the miniature golf. Perfectly priced for two!

❋ National D-Day Memorial ❋

Interested in seeing some historical and patriotic landmarks? You and your date will enjoy visiting the National D-Day Memorial. Located in Bedford, Virginia and surrounded by the scenic Blue Ridge Mountains, this memorial honors those who fought in World War II, and especially on D-Day in Normandy, France. Respect those who have fought for the freedom we hold dear today.

❋ Nottoway Plantation and Resort ❋

If you and your sweetheart are looking for a romantic getaway, consider the Nottoway Plantation and Resort! Tucked between Baton Rouge and New Orleans, Louisiana, this resort has something to offer for every occasion. Learn the history of the

1850s plantation owners, the Randolph family. The South's largest remaining antebellum museum, this is the perfect spot for your next office retreat, meeting, lover's getaway, or perhaps wedding destination!

✻ Pirate Ship Adventure ✻

Arrrgh matey, if you love the escapades of marauders past, take your date to a pirate ship adventure! See what the explorers and pirates of yesteryear would command to ransack the seas. With marauded merchant ships, and pirate's booty, you and your date will marvel at the loot carried away. Commandeer a spot on your adventure today!

✻ Planetarium ✻

Do you often dream about the stars? How about constellations? Then you may want to add snuggling with your date at the planetarium to your "to-do list." Enjoy the peacefulness of the faux night sky and the serenity of sitting quietly with your date under it. Be endearing and point out your date's zodiac.

✻ Polynesian Adventure Tour ✻

On your next visit to the Hawaiian Islands, take a Polynesian adventure tour! Take in the beautiful scenery of the islands. Visit a banana plantation and learn how this delicious fruit is grown and harvested. See the sights of Pearl Harbor and its rich and tumultuous history.

✻ Popcorn Palace ✻

There are more than just buttered and non-buttered options for you and your date. The Popcorn Palace, houses over 20 different flavors of popcorn! Mix and match flavors to create your own personalized tin. (Perfect keepsake of your date.) Take this opportunity to feed your date—it's sure to be a hit!

✻ Railroad Tunnel ✻

Flashlights?—Check! Maybe your date will appreciate a date through the railroad tunnel. Whether it is short with the light at the end, or long with no end in sight, these tunnels can be a treasure trove of history and geological anomalies. Make sure to point out the differences between the stalactite and stalagmite formations in the tunnels to really impress!

✻ St. Joseph's Plantation ✻

Are you and your date interested in some historical exploration? Then visit the St. Joseph's Plantation. Nestled in Vacherie, Louisiana, this family-owned plantation is one of the last remaining untouched sugar cane plantations around. Preserved in time, many of the original buildings have been left exactly how they were originally built. With over 2,500 acres (and a sister plantation, Felicity), there is plenty to explore in this scenic Southern tradition!

❈ Wilderness Adventure ❈

If you and your date are the rustic type, give a wilderness adventure a try! Hiking, rock climbing, and backpacking are only a few of the activities you can enjoy. Explore the great outdoors in a whole new way. Pack your camera, and capture the memories for a lifetime!

Indoors

❋ Air Museum ❋

If your special someone prefers to take to the skies on your next date, consider a trip to an air museum! Discover varying models of airplanes and aeronautical vehicles. Enrich your knowledge of the rich heritage of aeronautics! And once you're done exploring, end this romantic evening watching airplanes decorate the vast night sky.

❋ Art Museum ❋

If Picasso's blue period, Van Gogh's brushstrokes, or the Romanesque forced perspective movement are regular topics of conversation for you and your date, consider a trip to the art museum! Demonstrate the mastery of your brush strokes and techniques. Learn about the great masters and their contributions to the artistic community. Bring along a sketchbook and study the paintings and their intricacies. Sketch each other for a meaningful and romantic souvenir of the date!

❋ Atomic Testing Museum ❋

For an unforgettable experience, take your date to an atomic testing museum. A combination of science, history, and Area 51, this museum contains a plethora of information. Take a tour, and learn the ins and outs of rockets, and the history of atomic energy. This date is sure to be a blast!

❉ Ballet/Musicals ❉

If your date swoons over "The Black Swan" or "West Side Story", then perhaps you should take them to a ballet or musical! Admire the mastery of ballet and artistry of the dancers. Chuckle at the clever lyrics of the musical genre. Either way, when the curtain goes down, you will both be enthralled!

❉ Car Museum ❉

Hot Rods to Hot Wheels and a whole lot more—take your classy date to a classic car museum! Learn all about the history of automobiles, the updated features on snazzy new cars, and everything in between. Muse together about what it would have been like to live in the age of the Model T. Converse about each other's dream cars. This is a great way to find out your date's preferences and learn a little more about their personality.

❉ Corvette Museum ❉

While visiting the famous horse tracks of Kentucky, don't forget to race your date over to the Corvette museum! The Corvette is a classic, contemporary sports car that will never go out of style. Don't forget to bring your camera to capture the memories. This is the perfect place to hear engines roar, peruse dream cars, and get your heart racing!

❉ Cotton Museum ❉

If your relationship is growing stale—Take your date to a cotton museum, and find out how cotton grows from a seed to a plant. Uncover the subtle distinctions between planting and processing cotton. And be a softy and buy something from the gift shop on the way out—just make sure it's 100% cotton!

✺ CSI (Crime Scene Investigation) Museum ✺

Does Sherlock Holmes, Matlock, or Perry Mason fascinate you? Do you have an uncanny ability to solve murder mystery novels quickly? Then for an exciting twist, take your date to a CSI Experience exhibit! Attempt to solve your own simulated crime scene. Complete with suspects, victims, and clues, this is a date only the stealthiest private investigators can unravel! Surrounded by genuine forensic scientists, use the latest technology to capture the criminal mastermind before the night is over.

✺ Earth Science Museum ✺

Ever thought about taking your date to the earth science museum? Explore vast geographical anomalies such as the Grand Canyon, volcanoes, earthquakes, and other interesting earth facts. Learn how mining has changed the layout of the earth's surface, and how the process has evolved today. Find out what you can do to preserve the earth and how you can do your part to "Go Green".

✺ Go Kart Racing ✺

Ladies! Gentlemen! Start your engines! These machines might not hit NASCAR top speeds but you can still have a great time racing go karts on your next date. From slick track to classic karts there are a lot of options to try and you'll be surprised at the intensity of racing these small vehicles. Make sure to save time to have dinner or walk and talk afterward though. You don't want your whole date to be him or her leaving you in their dust on the track!

✳ Ice Skating ✳

Whether you play hockey, figure skate, or just like gliding leisurely along the ice, ice skating is a great way for you and your date to spend an evening together. Indoor rinks are open year round and you can bring your own skates or rent a pair on the cheap. Hold hands while skating around the rink or race up and down the length of the ice. Take turns skating patterns or words into the ice. See if you can work together to skate out the shape of a heart with your initials on it; it might just win you some brownie points!

✳ Indoor Surfing ✳

Do you love to surf? Freezing temperatures and chilly waters keeping you indoors? Or maybe you don't live by the ocean but still want to take your partner out for an adventurous date on the waves? Try indoor surfing! With classes to get you started and a variety of difficulty levels it won't matter if you're an experienced pro or just getting started, there is room for you both to have a great time. And if you don't feel comfortable standing on the waves try body boarding instead for an equally fun but slightly less challenging day.

✳ Laser Tag ✳

Tag, you're it! Couple up, for a laser tag double date. Most arenas require a minimum of four players, so split into two couples, take your date by the hand, and battle it out against your friends. Teamwork and strategy are a must if you are to win, and working together with your partner in mock combat is a great way for you both to bond and have fun too! Reenact your favorite movie battle scenes, become the hero and save your love from the enemy, and win bragging rights together.

✺ Lightner Museum ✺

Do you and your date have an appreciation for yore or yester-year's past? Then it's time for a trip to the Lightner Museum for an old-fashioned experience! Exquisite collections from the 19th and early 20th century are sure to make any antique connoisseur swoon. Take a tour through the elaborate treasuries, and marvel at the beautiful works of art and intricate carvings of craftsmen in past eras.

✺ Mechanical Museum ✺

Curious about what makes machines tick? If cogs and gears are your thing, treat your loved one to a date at the mechanical museum! Maybe even engineer a small working mechanism as a souvenir to take home! Add your own little something extra to make this date memorable.

✺ Museum of Sex ✺

What's more hot and steamy than sex? The Museum of Sex in New York is the perfect place to converse about an inevitable topic. Peruse beautiful photographs and artwork, discover the kinky habits of others, and learn about the history of sex (both human and animal!). It's sure to be an unforgettable experience.

✿ Osteology Museum ✿

The hip bone's connected to the thigh bone...and connect with your date after a visit to an osteology museum! This is the perfect place to discover how bone structure affects so much of the human (and animal) anatomy. Personalize the experience. Talk about the importance of a healthy diet and how it affects your bones. Don't forget to "bone" up on some lingo beforehand to impress your date with your osteology knowledge!

✿ Plant Museum ✿

Take your next date to the Henry B. Plant museum. Not just for houseplants, this museum showcases the building and construction of the Tampa Bay Motel. Visit the Grand Salon, Dining Room, and even the Flower House. Learn about the founder, railroad mogul Henry B. Plant.

✿ Railroad Museum ✿

Learning a bit about the locomotive history of our country can be an enriching experience, so take your next date to the railroad museum. Tour the exhibits that tell of the history of how our country was connected by the railroads and learn about the men who worked and died to make it happen. You both will leave with a deeper understanding of the rail system and a new topic of conversation you can both relate to. And make sure to get him or her a conductor's hat from the gift shop on the way out, just for fun!

❊ Spy Museum ❊

Love the 007 villains and movies the likes of "Argo"? Instead of going to the movies, why not take your date to the International Spy Museum? Explore interactive exhibits, and take pictures with classic spy gadgets. Brush up on your espionage knowledge, and learn a few new things along the way.

❊ Spotlight Theatres ❊

Do live dramas and entertainment sound exciting to you? Spotlight theatre could be just what you're looking for! These theaters are known for featuring local actors and encouraging children to be creative. Through song, dance, and other artistic forms of expression, you are sure to be entertained!

❊ Toy Museum ❊

Are you and your date a kid at heart? Relive your childhood at the toy museum! Discover which toys you both loved as kids, what toys your parents and grandparents may have played with, and explore the toys that the new generation will be enjoying and loving! Don't forget to stop by the gift shop on the way home and buy your date the toy they "always wanted" as a child — they will never forget the gesture!

❊ Wax Museum ❊

From Elvis to Nixon, James Dean to Jerry Lewis, you can see all your favorite stars, athletes, and historical figures up close and personal at the wax museum. This is a great opportunity to learn more about whom your date admires and who their heroes are. Point out your favorite Olympic athletes, presidents, and get a picture with movie stars of yesterday and today. It's a distinctive experience you both won't soon forget.

Indoor Sports Activities

✻ ½ hr. Couples Massage ✻

To unwind from a long day of outdoor activities or just to relax from a grueling week at work, take your date to the spa and book a half-hour couples massage. The dim lights, low music, and burning candles set a mood of tranquility where you both can melt away the worries and stresses of the week. Try a variety of techniques from hot stone to deep tissue massages and see what each of you prefer. What could be better than quietly lying together being pampered and relaxed?

✻ Arcade Bar ✻

The Mario Bros. have nothing on you and your date! For a fun change of pace, enjoy an exciting afternoon or evening clobbering ghouls or racing cars at an arcade bar. Get a few drinks and enjoy being an adult, while relishing feeling like a kid again. Don't forget your bag of quarters!

✻ Batting Cages ✻

No matter the time of year you can enjoy some baseball fun with your date without having to go to a major or minor league game. Slide into the batting cages to get in on the action yourselves! After warming up take turns seeing how many balls you can hit, or how far you can send them. There's no pressure or team competition, just a relaxed afternoon with you both enjoying a piece of America's favorite pastime.

❄ Billiards ❄

A couple games of billiards are something you and your date can enjoy at the bar or from the comfort of your own home. Whether it's a simple game of solids and stripes or the more strategic snooker this is a low-key way to enjoy some conversation and a little playful competition at the same time. Practice a few trick shots together and make it a recurring date so you can see your progress and have one more excuse to spend time with your loved one.

❄ Circus ❄

Do clowns, elephants, acrobats and other anomalies catch your fancy? Then treat your date to the circus! Feed peanuts to the elephants, marvel at the 5-legged donkey, and laugh at the hysterical antics of the clowns. Buy some cotton candy while you are watching the daring escapades of the acrobats, and don't forget to clap for the performers on your way out!

❄ Claddagh Dance Classes ❄

For your next date, try out a Claddagh dance class. Moving together will get you and your date closer to one another, while learning a new skill. In this situation, it's OK if you step on each other's toes. Enjoy dancing to beautiful Irish music. Perhaps end the night at an Irish pub to refresh yourselves after all of that exertion!

❄ Fencing ❄

En garde! If fencing and swordplay sound up your alley, take your date to a fencing lesson! Lunge like a Lancelot, feint like a Samurai, parry like you're in battle. Not sure you want to pick up a sword yourself? There are plenty of exhibitions where you both can enjoy watching other skillful fencers compete. This is sure to spice up your relationship!

❄ Ice Cream Emporium ❄

If you love variety and a bit of fun, take your date to an ice cream emporium. This is a wonderful place to sample a variety of flavors. With so many tasty creations, it will be hard to choose just one flavor, so make up a unique combination all your own! Don't forget to pick up a custom treat on the way out for something to remember your tasty night.

❄ Ice Skating ❄

Whether you play hockey, figure skate, or just like gliding leisurely along the ice, ice skating is a great way for you and your date to spend an evening together. Indoor rinks are open year round and you can bring your own skates or rent a pair on the cheap. Hold hands while skating around the rink or race up and down the length of the ice. Take turns skating patterns or words into the ice. See if you can work together to skate out the shape of a heart with your initials on it; it might just win you some brownie points!

✳ Improv Classes ✳

Do you or your date pride yourselves on having clever comebacks or dead-on impersonations? Then consider an improv class for your next outing. Improve upon your razor sharp wit and impeccable timing. Remember, dialogue is the key to a successful relationship.

✳ Martial Arts Exposition ✳

Are you a black, brown, or even white belt? Then take your next date to a martial arts exposition! Revel in the skill of other jujitsu, tae-kwon-do, and karate masters. Brush up on a few self-defense skills of your own. Gear up for a kicking good time!

✳ Mirror Maze ✳

Mirror mirror on the wall, who's the fairest of them all? The answer is, of course, your date! And if you both are looking for a unique and playful way to spend your next outing try navigating a mirror maze together. You'll need to keep ahold of each other's hands if you don't want to get turned around immediately. A mirror maze will twist and turn you around till you're not sure which of the reflections is the real you! It's not just a challenging mind game, but good fun and a way to goof off and be silly with your date.

✳ SkyZone ✳

Have you outgrown your childhood trampoline? Visit SkyZone's giant indoor trampoline! Take your next date to sky zone, and see what it's like to fly and bounce at the same time. Play basketball, time your slide, or just enjoy bouncing at this amazing trampoline park.

✳ Tapas Bar ✳

Are you dating a master chef? Then take them to a Tapas bar for a delicious evening. Sample Spanish Tapas, Mediterranean Tapas, or borrow Martha Stewart Tapas recipes. Customize this perfect event by creating your own Tapas recipe.

✳ Trampoline Park ✳

If you and your date are looking for some high octane fun that gets a good workout in on the side, check out a trampoline park. Trampoline parks have a variety of trampolines built into the floor and walls that allow you both to recapture the thrill of flying high you may have had as a kid in the backyard, but with a lot more room to play this time! Always wanted to dunk like an NBA player? Trampoline basketball courts allow you to soar like MJ or LeBron and perform dunk competition worthy slams. It's a unique and exciting way to have fun while getting in a great workout!

Outdoors

❀ Glow Golf ❀

Glow golf? That's right, night golf with balls that glow in the dark—of course! You and your date will love this out-of-the-ordinary entertainment. Watch out for the windmill!

❀ Historic Society ❀

Do you and your date love all things vintage and antique? Then take them to a historic society. Discover an array of hidden treasures to imbibe. See how the items are preserved to stand the test of time. Make sure your camera phone is handy, and recall your own memorable moments.

❀ Lion Country Safari ❀

Embrace your feline fetish? Take your date to a lion country safari! Observe the king of the jungle in his natural habitat. It's a surefire way to create amazing memories!

❀ Living Coast Discovery Center ❀

While visiting San Diego, take your date to the Living Coast Discovery Center. The knowledgeable staff will fill you in on the local animals, plants and habitats. With sharks, turtles and plenty of scenic trails, there won't be a shortage of things to see and discover!

❈ Miniature Golf ❈

Take time next weekend to enjoy spending time with your partner enjoying each other's company while participating in some fun activities. Head to your nearest beach resort for some fun in the sun and a few rounds of miniature golf on the side. The fun, low-stress environment of mini golf is a great way for you and your date to enjoy some friendly competition as you avoid windmills, sand traps, and other obstacles on the course. Afterwards kick off your shoes and spend time on the beach enjoying the cool evening air and gentle sounds of the waves. It's the perfect relaxing weekend getaway.

❈ Nature Park ❈

Take your date to a nature park. Beautiful scenery awaits you and your date. Stroll through gorgeous woods, cross peaceful streams, and let your inner explorer roam. This is a perfect date for lovers looking for conversation in beautiful surroundings.

❈ Oregon Gardens ❈

Botanical Gardens in Oregon? That's right—Look no further than the Oregon Gardens. You and your date will enjoy the awe-inspiring beauty of the flower gardens. Book a room at the resort, and spend a weekend unwinding, surrounded by the enchanting floral fragrances.

❋ Paintball ❋

Take your next date to a paintball fight. Choose your team, and load em' up! Whether you're in the woods or in the bunkers, you're bound to have a colorful time! Incorporate a friendly wager to up the ante!

❋ Philly Magic Gardens ❋

Are you and your date more avant-garde art lovers? Then don't miss the Philly Magic Gardens in Philadelphia. These gardens are the home of the works of the mosaic artist Isaiah Zagar. These eclectic, elaborate, outstanding works of art are guaranteed to inspire!

❋ Primate Sanctuary ❋

No need to go bananas for ideas for your next date! Take them to a primate sanctuary. Check out the monkeys, apes and gorillas while you're there. Not just for primates though, many sanctuaries house exotic birds, snakes, and other animals that can no longer be cared for by their owners.

❋ Round of Golf for Two ❋

Want a romantic, enjoyable afternoon? Round up your date for a round of golf. Rent a cart so you're not lugging your golf balls around, and enjoy relaxing in the scenic outdoors. Impress your date with a hole-in-one!

✻ Safari/Wildlife Adventure ✻

Do you and your date enjoy the great outdoors and seeing animals in their natural habitat? Suit up for your safari or wildlife adventure! Up close and personal, this experience is sure to bring out the wild side in each of you.

✻ Sunken Gardens ✻

Planning a visit to Florida? Make headway towards Florida's sunken gardens. Filled with exotic animals, beautiful foliage, and other sights, this would be perfect for a romantic date. The phenomenon of the Japanese gardens, butterfly garden, and cactus garden leave you awe inspired.

✻ Wildflower Center ✻

If you and your date are passing through Texas looking for a unique place to see wildflowers, look no further than the Lady Bird Johnson Wildflower Center. Named after the former first lady and actress Helen Hayes, this center was founded to protect and preserve botanical heritage. Don't forget to take your picture alongside the giant dragonfly sculpture!

✻ Wilderness Adventure ✻

If you and your date are the rustic type, give a wilderness adventure a try! Hiking, rock climbing, and backpacking are only a few of the activities you can go on. Explore the great outdoors in a whole new way. Oh, and uh—don't forget the camera!

We're going where?

✳ Archery Class ✳

Do you consider yourself a master of the bow and arrow? Or is it just something you have always wanted to do? Treat your date to some archery! Bring your own bow if you're just starting out, or opt for a private lesson. Set your aim on a goal, and fire away!

✳ Asana Climbing ✳

Suggest something new and unexpected with your date? Try out asana climbing. This unique exercise is sure to challenge you both. Whether you choose a gym, or explore the great outdoors, try something a little more unique than the ubiquitous treadmills.

✳ Biking Adventure for Two ✳

Prefer to explore on your own? Rent some bikes, and take your next date on a park bike tour. Tag alongside a tour guide to see the sights and scenery the park has to offer. Then travel, just the two of you, around to visit places you would otherwise never have gone!

✳ Corn Maze ✳

Do you enjoy getting lost with your date? Conjure up a visit to a corn maze. These intricate mazes, cut from mature cornfields, are the perfect way to spend a beautiful autumn afternoon. Try to follow the markers but don't stress about it, getting lost together could be half the fun!

❈ Equestrian Farm ❈

Searching for a peaceful date? Look no further than an equestrian farm. Converse with horse whisperers. Watch beautiful horses interact with each other. Perhaps take a trail ride through a beautiful woodland path.

❈ Funhouse Maze ❈

Stay close beside your partner during this date! Explore a funhouse maze. Fake walls, trick mirrors, this adventure is sure to twist and turn you around until you're not sure which way is up! Navigate your way to the end, and you ought to get a few laughs along the way.

❈ Ghost Tour ❈

If the paranormal sounds intriguing to you and your date, seek out a ghost tour. These ghoulish tours explore the history of hauntings, where apparitions have been witnessed!

❈ Historic Boat Tour ❈

Whether it's a Navy tug or a World War artifact—a historic boat tour may be the perfect smaller-scale adventure, to take your date. Across the country, you can find tours of boats that have ferried goods, people, and explorers across vast oceans. Tour boats that have stood guard and protected their regions of the sea from marauders.

❋ Laser Maze ❋

Laser maze anyone? Imagine that you are a super-spy while navigating the lasers. Practice your twisting and turning through the intricate connections. And whatever you do, don't hit the laser!

❋ Lighthouse Tour ❋

Take your next date on a lighthouse tour. Lighthouses are well-known for being a beacon of hope for ships that would otherwise be lost to the rocks or fog. At the heart of a lighthouse are its keeper and these people have interesting stories and histories to learn about. These brave souls had to keep a small light lit so that the colossal beam could shine. Just be prepared to walk up many flights of steps to get to the top!

❋ Park Sight Seeing Tour ❋

Do you love a local park, but don't know much about it? Have you ever thought about a park sight-seeing tour? Tour guides are readily available to reveal hidden treasures located throughout the park. From breathtaking views to quiet, peaceful trails, there is sure to be something for everyone.

❋ Pioneer Farms ❋

Wish you had a time machine? Pioneer Farms Living History Park is the blast from the past you've been looking for, including live theatre. Ask questions about the time period, and see what it was like to live way back when.

❋ Pumpkin Patch ❋

When the temperature falls and the leaves start to change color, where is the best place to take your date? A pumpkin patch, of course! Take a hay ride through the luscious autumn colors, and try your hand at carving a pumpkin. Don't forget to bundle up!

❋ Pirate Ship Adventure ❋

Arrrgh matey, if you love the escapades of marauders past, take your date to a pirate ship adventure! This seaside cruise adventure is the perfect blend of relaxation fused with entertainment. Bon voyage!

❋ Rosse Posse Acre Tour ❋

Have you ever wanted to see and touch an elk up close? At Rosse Posse Acres, you can! Take the tour with your date and see these beautiful creatures in a whole new light. Be sure to say hi to one of the adorable miniature schnauzers that also call this elk farm home!

❋ Trolley Tour ❋

Do you prefer to know as much about your vacation locale as possible? Then take your date on a trolley tour. Listen as the tour guide explains the history and significance of buildings and places. Sit back and relax, and give your feet a rest after trekking through a new city!

❀ Warrior Fit Boot Camp ❀

Ready to push yourself to the limit? See how far you can run, lift, and keep up with others around you? Then you and your date should make a date—to get fit! Join a warrior fit boot camp, specifically centered around Marine-style fitness. With camps across the country, there is surely one to pique your interest.

❀ Waterfalls ❀

Watch as the crisp, cool water cascades into the basin below. Scenic waterfalls are the perfect stage for any date. Explore a hiking trail to travel, perhaps even behind the shimmering sheet of water. Tag along with a tour guide to learn about the history of the particular falls. Bring along your camera for some amazing photographs!

❀ Wildlife Ranch ❀

Itching for a little excitement on your next date? Seek out a wildlife ranch! Resplendent in the variety of animals you can encounter, this date won't be lacking for interesting things to do and see. Feed some of the animals, learn about their habits and care, there's so much to do, you won't want to leave!

Sporting Events

❀ Endurocross ❀

If you and your date like racing, stunts, and jumps then grab tickets to your next Endurocross event. Mixing endurance racing with obstacles and jumps, this dirt bike challenge pits riders on an indoor course built to test their skill and strength. The variety of obstacles and challenges keeps it fresh and entertaining, and the unpredictability and danger of the course adds just the right amount of adrenaline pumping excitement! Get ready to get loud! It's a great way to enjoy some thrilling fun on your next date!

❀ Ice Hockey ❀

Cheer on your home team with your date at your city's next ice hockey game. From the loud, adrenaline pumped crowd to the excitement of the fast-paced on ice action, a hockey game is a thrilling experience for you and your date to enjoy together. Whether it's an NHL game or a minor league team the environment is loud, the energy is high, and you both will be out of your seats cheering and screaming with a passion!

❀ MLB Stadium Seats ❀

Nothing is more traditionally American than a game of baseball, and you and your date can have a great time enjoying America's favorite pastime at your next home major league baseball game. The crack of the bat, the snap of the ball in the glove, the smell and sound of peanuts and cotton candy; everything at the ball field evokes nostalgia and celebrates the competitive spirit. Through the slower innings take a walk around the concourse and see some of the historical landmarks of the stadium, or stop by the 500 Club for a drink. It's all about taking in the whole experience and spending a relaxed evening with your date.

❋ Minor League Sporting Event ❋

(Major League/High School Sporting Events can be used interchangeably with Minor League Sporting Events).

❋ NBA Stadium Seats Game Day ❋

Put on your favorite player's jersey and lace up your sneakers, it's time to head to the stadium with your date for NBA game day. Get there early for a pregame show with the mascot performing acrobatic dunks and tricks. Take a tour of the stadium and see some of the history of your team and its greatest players. And when tipoff comes get ready to chant, clap, and cheer your team on through every three pointer and slam dunk!

By the Bay

❀ Adventure Diving ❀

Is scuba diving a little too tame for you and your date's tastes? Up the challenge with adventure diving. You can go night-diving or explore ship or boat wrecks and take underwater pictures. But before you two resurface, don't forget to take selfies with the fish—you could get some very interesting results!

❀ Aquarena Center ❀

Would you two want to experience the wonders of water and its ecosystems without necessarily getting in it? The Aquarena Center features glass-bottom-boat educational tours daily on Spring Lake, which has the United States' densest turtle population. The center features the famous 1,000 gallon aquarium. But don't forget to look up: the center is located within a high-traffic flight circuit for migrating birds.

❀ Casino Cruise ❀

What do you get when you combine the luxuriousness of a cruise with the fun of a casino? A casino cruise! Your date will love this scenic and fun-filled weekend. There are plenty of bars and pubs on-board to choose from—from library bars to sports bars and everything in-between. Watch seaside theatre, play mini-golf on deck, go to the spa, or try your luck at the blackjack or craps table.

✹ Catamaran Cruise ✹

Take your next date on a Catamaran Cruise. Sail aboard the picturesque "Lady Joana". Explore the waters of Costa Brava with snorkeling, diving, and even a water trampoline. With snacks and beverages of your choice, enjoy a fun-filled sunny day, before having to go back to the island.

✹ Deep Sea Fishing ✹

Looking for a tuna or swordfish for dinner tonight? Instead of heading to the grocery store, head out into the sea to catch your dinner with some deep sea fishing! This is a much more rugged endeavor than normal fishing so if you aren't experienced make sure to book passage with a captain and guide who know the waters and the techniques. But nothing is more thrilling than the accomplishment of wrangling a large tuna or mackerel into the boat. Dinner is served!

✹ Dining Cruise ✹

Maybe you're thinking about taking your date out for a meal but want something with a little more "oomph." A dining cruise is an exciting alternative to a regular restaurant. Book tickets during a holiday in a locale that will be featuring fireworks for a thrilling, unique dinner-and-a-show. Or you two can simply relax to the accompaniment of the lapping water and the cruise's featured musicians.

✻ Hornblower Cruise ✻

For your next date, take to the seas with a Hornblower Cruise! A San Francisco based Yacht Company, Hornblower Cruises owns eight ports, so there will be plenty of options from which to choose. Visit Lake Tahoe, Alcatraz, or even Liberty Island on this romantic ocean getaway. Don't forget to bring along your camera to take pictures of the sights, and maybe even spot some marine life along the way!

✻ Hydro Biking ✻

If you want a low-impact, fun, water-based activity, you and your partner should try hydro biking. The relaxing repetition of cycling, the tranquility of water, and the teamwork needed to navigate the bike can enrich your quality time with your best friend. Hydro biking can also be a great group activity if you two want other couples to participate. You might even get to be eye-level with the local waterfowl and see the world from a new perspective.

✻ Manatee Tour and Diving ✻

Perhaps one or both of you want to learn more about an endangered species to help protect. Maybe you even want to interact with a marine animal, but, for any given reason, dolphins just don't interest you or your love? Manatees are a friendly alternative, and Florida is the hotspot for manatee tours and dives. Swim with, pet, and learn about these laid-back, endangered creatures.

✿ Ocean Explorer Cruise ✿

Do you and your partner have sea legs to stretch but want a little more adventure than a beach-side resort might offer? An ocean explorer cruise can give you a chance to swim, surf, and rock climb, attend concerts or variety shows. You could not ask for a more romantic evening looking at an expansive ocean sunset followed by stargazing while being relaxed by the ship's rocking. Also, if you want to go with other couples but want occasional relaxing downtime with your sweetie without anyone else being left with nothing to do, a cruise is perfect.

✿ Riverboat Cruise ✿

Are you both eager to travel on a boat but perhaps uncomfortable being far away from shore? A riverboat cruise solves the quandary. Riverboats offer the opportunities to learn the history of the river—where there is water, there are civilizations that thrive—and encounter the culture that draws life from the waters. Many riverboats lines also feature themed cruises, exquisite dining, and live entertainment.

✿ Scuba Diving ✿

Would you both like to escape the noise and brightness of land-life for a while? Scuba diving takes you to a glimmering, relaxed, quiet world, gives you fantastic, low-impact exercise, and offers up-close and personal meetings with exotic fishes. Depending on your respective skill levels, you two could dive and swim in a lake, a bay, or the ocean. You may not discover treasure, but the memories you make together will be priceless.

✼ Sportfishing ✼

For an activity that is a bit more challenging spend the day on the water with your date sportfishing. Local competitions aren't hard to find and you can enjoy all the serenity of a day on the water while still injecting some spice into the day with some friendly competition. Or for a simple and relaxing time together just grab your fishing poles and lie out lazily on the dock, boat, or shore without a care in the world waiting for a bite. This is a great time to talk and bond together and if you bring home dinner that night, all the better!

✼ Whale Watching Cruise ✼

Some people are happy to take others' at their word that whales are huge. But maybe you and your companion want to see these aquatic giants for yourselves! Learn about whales, numerous other types of marine life, and the environmental efforts to preserve them. The air tends to be cooler out on the water than on land, so your whale watching cruise might give the two of you some cuddle time while waiting for the whales!

A free eBook edition is available with the purchase of this book.

To claim your free eBook edition:

1. Download the Shelfie app.
2. Write your name in uppser case in the box.
3. Use the Shelfie app to submit a photo.
4. Download your eBook to any device.

Shelfie

A free eBook edition is available
with the purchase of this print book.

CLEARLY PRINT YOUR NAME ABOVE IN UPPER CASE

Instructions to claim your free eBook edition:
1. Download the Shelfie app for Android or iOS
2. Write your name in **UPPER CASE** above
3. Use the Shelfie app to submit a photo
4. Download your eBook to any device

Print & Digital Together Forever.

Snap a photo

Free eBook

Read anywhere

The Morgan James
Speakers Group

↗ www.TheMorganJamesSpeakersGroup.com

We connect Morgan James published
authors with live and online events
and audiences whom will benefit
from their expertise.